"It is always such an encouragement when you watch someone put their hand in the hand of God and walk in faith's obedience. It makes you want to do the same, to live life on faith's higher plane. Terry's varied experiences in her God Adventure, from rape to a broken marriage to the adoption of not one but three daughters, will deeply touch your heart. This is a faith builder!"

"I have long admired Terry Meeuwsen for her passion, courage, and determination to follow God. In *The God Adventure,* Terry invites us to join her in the really deep water. As we truly listen to her story and her heart, the invitation does not frighten us. It pulls us forward—and courage bubbles up in our own hearts until we, too, are determined not to miss God's moment."

"Terry Meeuwsen shows through personal stories that walking with Jesus is a contin⋯ ᵃdventure. He came that 'we may have life, and ⊦ ᵃantly.' Terry encourages us to launch ⸳ ᵉcause when we do, we wiⅼⅼ ⸳ ⸳undant adventure with H⸳

"In *The God Adventure*, Terry Meeuwsen brings a fresh, practical perspective to the life of faith. With neither a hint of judgment, nor a rose-colored view, Terry reignites the dream within, reminding us that today is God's perfect plan to lead us to the tomorrow He has promised."

MARILYN HICKEY
PRESIDENT AND FOUNDER,
MARILYN HICKEY MINISTRIES

# THE
# GOD
## *Adventure*

# TERRY
# MEEUWSEN

Multnomah® Publishers *Sisters, Oregon*

THE GOD ADVENTURE
published by Multnomah Publishers, Inc.

© 2004 by Terry Meeuwsen
International Standard Book Number: 1-59052-250-8

Cover image by Betsie Van der Meer / Getty Images

Italics in Scripture are the author's emphasis.
Unless otherwise indicated, Scripture quotations are from:
*The Holy Bible,* New International Version © 1973, 1984 by International Bible Society,
used by permission of Zondervan Publishing House
Other Scripture quotations are from:
*The Holy Bible,* English Standard Version (ESV) © 2001 by Crossway Bibles,
a division of Good News Publishers. Used by permission. All rights reserved.
*New American Standard Bible*®(NASB) © 1960, 1977, 1995
by the Lockman Foundation. Used by permission.
*The Holy Bible,* New King James Version (NKJV) © 1984 by Thomas Nelson, Inc.
*The Amplified Bible* (AMP) © 1965, 1987 by Zondervan Publishing House.
*Holy Bible,* New Living Translation (NLT) © 1996.
Used by permission of Tyndale House Publishers, Inc. All rights reserved.
*The Message* by Eugene H. Peterson, Copyright © 1993, 1994, 1995, 1996, 2000.
Used by permission of NavPress Publishing Group. All rights reserved.
*The New Testament in Modern English,* Revised Edition (Phillips)
© 1958, 1960, 1972 by J. B. Phillips
*Contemporary English Version* (CEV) © 1995 by American Bible Society

*Multnomah* is a trademark of Multnomah Publishers, Inc., and is registered in the U.S. Patent and
Trademark Office. The colophon is a trademark of Multnomah Publishers, Inc.

Printed in the United States of America

For information:
MULTNOMAH PUBLISHERS, INC. • P.O. BOX 1720 • SISTERS, OREGON 97759

Library of Congress Cataloging-in-Publication Data

Meeuwsen, Terry Anne.
The God adventure / by Terry Meeuwsen.
p. cm.
ISBN 1-59052-250-8
1. Christian life. I. Title.
BV4501.3.M44 2005
248.4—dc22

2004022615

05 06 07 08 09 10—10 9 8 7 6 5 4 3 2 1 0

# Dedication

This book is dedicated with love to
my four oldest children—
Drew, Tory, J. P., and Tyler—
who bravely chose to say yes to a
God adventure that they knew
would change each of them and our family forever…
…and to my three new daughters—
Alysa, Zoya, and Sophia—
who had the courage to walk away
from everything familiar
into a whole new life with people they barely knew…
…and to Andy, my husband and treasured friend,
whose willingness to hear God's voice
and follow His leading
has made all the difference in my life
and in the life of our family.

# Contents

# Foreword

It is amazing how a sovereign God can take a life that has been bruised and broken and turn it into something beautiful for His glory.

In every life, there is a God adventure just waiting to unfold. The secret is whether you are willing to listen to the voice of God, trust Him, and then step out into the arms of the One who not only holds the future, but is Himself the future.

In this remarkable book, Terry opens her heart to tell of a brutal rape and a failed marriage to an alcoholic husband. Out of this has come the radiant life of a loving, mature woman who has understanding, compassion, and great wisdom.

There are few who, when faced with a busy schedule of nationwide television appearances, would reach out to share a family's love with three sisters from a Ukrainian orphanage, who longed for a family to adopt them. How Terry wound up adding three lovely young daughters to her family, and how she has made a life with her beloved husband, Andy, will not only warm your heart but also bring to you a clear application of timeless scriptural truths.

*Pat Robertson*

# Acknowledgments

Writing a book is a labor of love. It is a journey of ups and downs, inspiration and frustration. No sane person embarks on this journey alone. Working with Multnomah has been genuinely wonderful. Thank you, Don Jacobson, Bill Jensen, David Webb, and all of you for catching the vision for this book from the get-go. David Kopp, your gentle encouragement was a perfect catalyst. Kimberly Brock, Kristina Coulter, Penny Whipps, thanks to you and the marketing team for your creativity and commitment to excellence. Larry Libby, editor extraordinaire, your enthusiasm, vision for, and commitment to this message made all the difference. Thank you for pouring yourself into this with gusto. I loved working with you.

At CBN I have the privilege of working every day with several remarkable men. I want to thank Pat and Gordon Robertson for hearing my heart and encouraging and supporting me and my family through our recent Ukrainian adventure. Michael Little, president of CBN, also stood with us and said, "Go!" It's an honor to work with all of you; it's a privilege to call you friends.

Finally, I want to acknowledge and thank my

friend and personal assistant, Rhonda Palser. She is the glue that held this project together, kept it in process, and saw that it made it to completion. Her gifts and abilities bless me every day, but it is her quiet, gentle reflection of Jesus I appreciate most.

# A Word from the Author

This book is not an autobiography, though I have shared many personal experiences from my own life. What is it, then? I'd like to call it an invitation to engage in a way of living that makes every day an adventure, every challenge an opportunity to know Him more completely. This invitation comes with an RSVP. I hope your answer will be "yes!"

# What Is a
# God Adventure?

*"Today, if you hear his voice,*
*do not harden your hearts."*

HEBREWS 4:7

1

I REMEMBER as a teenager watching the popular television action series *Mission: Impossible*. Every episode began with a secret agent and a tape. The anonymous recorded voice would say, *"Your mission, should you choose to accept it, is..."* And then the mysterious spymaster would describe some wild and dangerous assignment, with little chance of success or survival.

The agent always chose to accept the challenge. I can't ever remember him turning it down. Well, of course. It would put a bit of a damper on the episode if the hero said, "Are you kidding? Are you crazy? A guy could get hurt doing stuff like that!" and then just walked away.

But thankfully the spy always said yes, launching all of us in TV Land into an hour (minus commercials) of fast cars, dangerous women, exploding attaché cases, and daring deeds.

There is a parallel, I believe, with what God offers His sons and daughters throughout our lives. At various points along the way (you never know when) God opens the door to unique experiences, opportunities, and challenges. Like the spy in *Mission: Impossible,* we can choose to accept these undertakings, these callings, or we can walk away.

The choice is real. You can walk on the adventure side of life and be an individual God selects for urgent kingdom missions, or you can close the door and close your life to experiences and memories that might have been yours—but now never will be.

## IF YOU DON'T, SOMEONE WILL

There's an intriguing bit of dialogue in the book of Esther that stands out to me each time I read it. Esther is the only book in Scripture that never mentions God's name even once—and yet you see the hand of God at every turn in the narrative.

You probably remember Esther's amazing rags-to-riches story. She was a beautiful Jewish girl in Susa, the capital city of Persia, in a day when the Medo-Persian Empire ruled the world. Selected to become the replacement queen in a nationwide beauty pageant, Esther had to leave her home, and Mordecai, her uncle who had raised her. Now established in the royal palace as queen, she learned of an evil plot to destroy all the Jews across the empire. Mordecai heard about it, too, and in great distress sent an urgent message to Esther. He urged her to approach the king and plead for the life of her people.

But Esther hesitated.

Who wouldn't? The penalty for entering the king's presence without a specific invitation was death. (I wonder how he would have handled telemarketers calling during the dinner hour?) Under extraordinary circumstances, the king might extend his golden scepter and spare the petitioner's life—but the prospects of taking that sort of chance were terrifying.

The young queen reported all these things in a message to her guardian, and he sent back this word...this small slice of dialogue I can't get out of my mind.

> "Do not think in your heart that you will escape in the king's palace any more than all the other Jews. For if you remain completely silent at this time, relief and deliverance will arise for the Jews from another place, but you and your father's house will perish. Yet who knows whether you have come to the kingdom for such a time as this?"
>
> ESTHER 4:13–14, NKJV

Notice the second sentence in Mordecai's message: *"For if you remain completely silent at this time, relief and deliverance will arise for the Jews from another place."* In other words, Mordecai was saying, "I have faith that the God of our fathers will not allow His people to be totally destroyed in this way. Somehow, He will step in. Somehow, He will spare a remnant of His people. If you sit back and remain silent, Esther, God will use someone else to achieve His purposes. But you are His first choice, and it's up to you how you're going to respond."

Esther, of course, took her uncle's message to heart. She determined to step into this God adventure—this opportunity to save her people. After calling all the Jews in the city to fast and pray for her, the young woman said, "And so I will go to the king, which is against the law; and if I perish, I perish!" (v. 16, NKJV).

When God wants something done, when He has some kingdom "mission impossible" to accomplish, He goes looking for a man or woman to take the assignment. The Bible tells us that "the eyes of the LORD move to and fro throughout the earth that He may strongly support those whose heart is completely His" (2 Chronicles 16:9, NASB).

He's looking for people who will take on risky operations of love and mercy. He is looking for men and women who will put His will above everything else in life. And every now and then, perhaps even today, His eye rests on you, and He offers you that opportunity.

You can take it, or you can let it go by. If you don't do it, He'll probably select someone else—"relief and deliverance will arise...from another place"—and the job will get done. *But you won't even be able to imagine what you've missed!*

## A FORK IN THE ROAD

Another story that haunts me is Jesus' encounter with a nameless wealthy young man as He made His final journey toward Jerusalem.

Here was an important civic leader, a youthful climber with prestige, bearing, and a bank account that would have been the envy of many older men in Judea. But there was a hollowness in his chest that led him ever so close to the God adventure of a lifetime.

For all his status and personal wealth, this man had a hungry heart. The Gospel of Mark tells us that he *ran* to Jesus, falling on his knees in the dust before Him. You know the story. He asked Jesus what he had

*The God Adventure*

to do to inherit eternal life. He knew the commands, and he'd kept them all since he was a boy.

But there was something more, and he knew it. He deeply wanted that something. But with all his heart? Not quite.

Mark tells us that Jesus looked at him and loved him.

> "One thing you lack," he said. "Go, sell everything you have and give to the poor, and you will have treasure in heaven. Then come, follow me."
>
> MARK 10:21

It was a wide-open invitation into a God adventure from the lips of God's Son. *"Your mission, should you choose to accept it...."* We know that he didn't accept the mission. We know that he "went away sad" (v. 22). The original language seems to indicate that this was something more than feeling a little down. He grieved. His heart was very heavy. Everything in him told him he was making a wrong choice...but he made it anyway. Jesus wasn't asking him for his money. He wanted to change his identity. He was inviting him into a new way of life. It's quite a picture, isn't it? That invitation is still extended to each of us today.

But what if he'd made a different choice? What if this young man whom Jesus loved so dearly had taken a deep breath, agreed to the Lord's terms, went back to his beautiful villa, and sold everything he owned except the clothes on his back? What if he had turned those assets over to a steward with the instructions to distribute everything, right down to the last denarius, to the poor people in the towns and villages across Judea? Then let's imagine he came running back to Jesus, fell at His knees again, and said, "Teacher, it's done. Everything's gone. Everything's sold. Lead me, Lord!"

What would his life have been like from that point on?

We can't know that, of course. But maybe we can speculate a little. Would he have savored the close companionship of God's Messiah, as Jesus walked toward Jerusalem and Calvary? Would he have become disciple #13, and then one of the mighty apostles, carrying the word of Christ out into the frontiers of civilization? Would he have experienced the very power of God flowing through him, healing the sick, raising the dead, and opening prison doors? Might he have written a book of the Bible that would touch billions of lives over thousands of years? Would his name have appeared on the foundation stones of the New Jerusalem, in place of Judas (Revelation 21:14)?

And then what of eternity?

Jesus specifically told the wealthy young man that he would have treasure in heaven. To who else did He reveal such a thing? No one! When had Jesus ever spoken directly to an individual about his or her eternal destiny on the Other Side?

Something unimaginably significant awaited this young man…if only he would have responded in that moment, at that fork in the road. When the One who created the glories of the universe and set galaxies spinning into the void tells you He has something special in mind for you, well…who can even conceive of such a thing?

It was all right there for this young man. A life of transcendent joy and purpose. It was all within reach at the crossroads that day.

And he just walked away. He refused the offer. *"At this the man's face fell. He went away sad"* (v. 22).

And I have to believe that for the rest of his hollow days, until he was an old, old man, he would remember that moment, remember those eyes that met his, eyes that seemed to open into an eternal vastness…and he would ask himself how it might have been if he had traded in his gold for Jesus.

The point is, we have no idea—not even the smallest notion—of what we are accepting or what we are refusing when we make a choice about a God adventure. The implications reach across the years of this life and send their reverberations into eternity.

Since we'll never know, the wise choice is to always follow God, no matter what He asks, no matter where He leads.

Even if it's to a cross.


## A Bigger Perspective

For years I chose not to participate in God adventures by simply not choosing at all. That's a decision, too. Not choosing *is* a choice.

Not long ago, we had former NBA great David Thompson on the *700 Club,* talking about coming to Christ after years of superstardom in the incredibly bright spotlight of professional sports. As with so many other athletes in that intoxicating realm, David pursued pleasure and became involved in many things he shouldn't have. By his own account, he was really all about himself in those days.

In the interview, he used the word *EGO* as an acronym for *Edging God Out.* And so it is for all of us. When we steadfastly close our hearts to God's invitations, when we neglect to acknowledge His presence in our lives, we're pretty much living in an "ego" mode, edging God out simply by staying in the center of our own universe. After years of living that way, it becomes more and more difficult to see things from a bigger perspective.

I think we're born staring at our navels—and continue to live that way until we hear the voice of God speak to us in some fashion, through some channel or avenue, and we say yes to a deeper walk with Him. Now that might sound soft, warm, and spiritual, but it can be very frightening. It's not without a price tag. But the blessings—both here and in the world to come— far, far outweigh that price tag. And once you get a taste of walking with Him, living with Him, hearing from Him, and being empowered by Him, nothing else will ever satisfy you again.

## "ONE MORE THING"?

Perhaps as you read these words, you're thinking, *This sounds good. A God adventure may be just what I need in my life.* Then again, the thought of adding "one more thing" to an already overcrowded schedule might strike terror in your heart. You may already feel on the verge of losing control to a schedule that is trying to swallow you alive.

It's true that as believers we war against principalities and powers in the spirit realm—and I would never make light of that. But we also war against cell phones, fax machines, deadlines, homework, soccer schedules, and a seemingly endless list of commitments and distractions in our lives. It is so easy to get in the mode where life runs us, rather than the other way around. It's all going by so fast that we can almost feel the wind on our faces as time flies by.

If I could give a peek inside my apprehensions and worries, this one rates pretty high. I don't want to go through life having my life live me. I want to stand fully in the midst of it all on the rock of Truth and make choices that cause my life to matter.

Yes, it's a constant battle. But I can tell you this: If the pace and busyness of life has overwhelmed me to the point that I can't respond to the call of God—or even hear His voice—something has gone terribly wrong. Perhaps the reason some of us never hear the summons to a God adventure is because we never give Him a minute of our time. He can't get a word in edgewise. His still, small voice is drowned out by turmoil and noise. The psalmist writes of a proud, arrogant

*The God Adventure*

individual who was so full of himself that "in all his thoughts there is no room for God" (Psalm 10:4). May that never, never be said of me!

No room for God? No heart for God adventures? Why else are we here? Why else are we alive?

I think it must grieve God so deeply that He has prepared such an incredible journey and adventure for us during our years on earth, and so many of us choose not to tap into it. Sometimes we treat God as if He's there for our convenience—as if He's some kind of celestial Santa Claus.

We had an e-mail sent to the *700 Club* last week from a lesbian. She wrote to Pat Robertson and said, "You're critical of my lifestyle as a homosexual, and yet since I've come out of the closet I'm so happy. Isn't my happiness what it's all about? Isn't this what matters to God?"

I don't think this woman's reasoning is all that unusual these days. Many people—including Christians—have bought into this creed. Isn't my happiness the most important thing? Isn't this what God's interested in above all else? I'm *supposed* to be happy, aren't I? Isn't this what life is all about?

No, as a matter of fact, it isn't. God's primary interest is not in our happiness. He's interested in our knowing Him, obeying Him, loving Him, being shaped by Him, and getting over the finish line to spend eternity with Him. At different points in life, we've probably all railed at God, saying, *Why did You allow this to happen? Why didn't You give me what I asked You and pleaded with You for? Why do You leave me in this terrible situation? Can't You see it's breaking my heart?* The ironic thing is that in the midst of difficult, heart-wrenching circumstances, we find Him in a deeper, more profound way than ever before. We find His presence and His strong help. We experience His comfort, provision, and whispered encouragements. And little by little, joy begins to seep into our soul—in ways we could have never known apart from those trying situations.

So often we allow ourselves to be content with the tiniest fraction of what God intended us to experience. We talk *about* God more than we talk *to* Him. We passively participate in the adventures of others—in stories of adventures—rather than living those adventures with Him.

There is more to life than this.

There are real-life rescue missions behind enemy lines. There are captives to be found and released. There are doors that will open at the most extraordinary times in the most extraordinary places. There are voyages of faith and expeditions of God-supplied courage with your name on them…should you choose to accept them.

Yes, the job will get done one way or another, with or without you. The eyes of the Lord, roving to and fro throughout the earth, will find someone else to step into the gap He had intended for you.

Don't let it happen! Don't walk away sad and live out your life with that most desolate of companions…

*What might have been.*

Throwing caution to the wind and choosing to live outside my comfort zone wasn't something I just randomly decided to do one day. God's invitation to come "out into the deep" with Him actually came at one of the lowest points in my life.

# The River of Life

*"Launch out into the deep and*
*let down your nets for a catch."*

LUKE 5:4, NKJV

2

SIRENS WAILED in the night and seemed to be drawing closer. I sat alone in the darkness in the rocker next to the window, bundled in my robe.

Were the sirens for him? What if he'd had too much to drink and hit a pole or ran off the road? Worse yet…what if he hit and injured someone else? *Oh God, please protect him, and protect others from him.*

The sirens trailed off. I rocked back and forth, a deep sadness upon me. How did I get here? What was happening to my marriage? What should I do? At 3 A.M. I finally climbed into bed, exhausted and confused. It was an evening that would repeat itself many times over the next several years.

How had I, Terry Meeuwsen, happy small-town girl and former Miss America, come to such a place…sitting in a rocker, looking out into the darkness, my heart so near despair?

## From Lounge Singer to Minstrel

In my hometown in the Midwest, everybody knew everybody. As you might imagine, being raised in such a place was both a blessing and a challenge! The "blessing" part of it was spending your childhood days in a town where people cared about each other, were kind to each other, knew each other's struggles, and helped each other out. In many ways, it was a great place to grow up. But that was something I wouldn't recognize for many long years.

From the time I was a small child, I'd always loved performing. I grew up going to movies like *The King and I, South Pacific, The Sound of Music,* and *The Ten Commandments*. It had always been my dream to be a singer and an actress. I took voice lessons, dance classes, and eventually got involved in small college productions right there in my hometown.

Over the years, however, culture changed—and the movies along with it. By the time I was out of school, theaters were filled with movies like *Joe, Easy Rider,* and *They Shoot Horses, Don't They?* The hopelessness and fatalism in these movies was a far cry from the messages of life and inspiration I'd seen as a child.

My first break into the professional entertainment world came in the late sixties, when I was nineteen years old and began singing in big-city nightclubs. Oh, I felt so *glamorous*. I imagined that I was "on my way" to accomplishing all my dreams in life. I pursued my career in earnest, doing all those things I thought I needed to do and paying all those dues I thought I needed to pay. My self-confidence was more than halfway to cockiness; nobody was going to stand in my way or stop me.

Raised as I was in a very conservative family, I saw things in that nightclub world that clashed violently with the solid Midwest values of my parents and my youth. Those feelings nagged at me a bit, creating some disquiet in the back rooms of my heart. But overwhelming all such hesitations was the giddy sensation that I had *arrived!* I felt so important being caught up in this "sophisticated" world of adults and alcohol and professional music that I looked past all the darker aspects of this lifestyle. I told myself, *I can deal with this.* And I pressed on to the goal I had set for myself.

To be perfectly honest, God really wasn't a part of the equation in those days. It wasn't that I ruled Him out. I really just didn't have time for Him. I was too busy pursuing my dreams.

After working in the nightclub scene for a while, I

had a chance to join a pop singing group called the
New Christy Minstrels. I had never traveled anywhere
alone, but the day came when I found myself boarding
a jet for Los Angeles, certain that this was my "big
break." Though our group's home office was in L.A.,
we lived out of our suitcases for months on end. The
occasional nightclub gigs of a week or two were a wel-
come relief from the endless one-night gigs at concerts,
fairs, colleges, and special events. We traveled domesti-
cally and internationally, performing at all kinds of
venues and under all manner of circumstances. It was
a crash course on life in the fast lane.

Though I'd been raised in a Christian denomination, I'd never read the Bible and didn't know anything
about inviting Christ into my life. I guess I thought
you were born into your faith. My parents were members of a Christian denomination, so I supposed that
made me a Christian, too. I had been baptized and
confirmed (once upon a time), but felt no personal
responsibility in any of it.

The longer I was on my own and away from my
folks, the further I wandered from any established set
of values. I never consciously turned away from God; I
just never thought about Him. To paraphrase David's
words in Psalm 10:4, "In all my thoughts, there was no
room for God." If He existed at all, He seemed *very* far

away—and hardly relevant. I was completely caught up in my career and my goals.

In the middle of one of our longer, more grueling tours, the New Christy Minstrels were performing in Honolulu, Hawaii, with headliner Don Ho. And in that lovely place of long beaches and soft tropical breezes, my life suddenly turned upside down and was never the same again.

## VULNERABILITY AND FEAR

The very last night that we were in Hawaii, I accepted an invitation from an employee of the club where we had been performing. He offered to take me around for an hour or two and show me some of the other clubs in town.

*Well, why not?* I thought. *It'll be fun.* So I accepted his invitation. As the day began to wane, however, it dawned on me that we were leaving the next day and I desperately needed to pack and get organized. I wanted so badly to call this man back and say, "Thanks so much for the invitation, but I really can't go tonight."

I wish with all my heart I had done that.

But I didn't want him to take it as a personal rejection, so I decided to follow through with our plans and do my packing late that night.

Traveling around town, my escort was polite and friendly. We were both staying in the same hotel, where the club was, and when we finally got back around 1:30 A.M., he invited me to his room for a drink.

I said no, that I couldn't do that and I needed to pack. But as the elevator arrived at my floor and the door opened, he reached his arm across the open doorway and said, "Come on. Just one drink."

Rather than create a big scene, I said, "Okay. One drink. And then I've *really* got to get moving."

I sat on the couch while he went into the kitchen to get our drinks. I was just sitting there, looking out the window, and the next thing I knew this man was on top of me. And that night was the night I experienced a violent two-and-a-half-hour rape.

It took me a long time in the months that followed to even use that word, *rape*. It was such a raw sounding word, and it made me feel so vulnerable to say it. Life changed for me that night. Suddenly, it wasn't so easy to order my life into sweet little compartments and easy definitions. It was no longer safe to trust people. I realized that I could not control my life or my circumstances. I felt so very alone, and the years

*The River of Life*

stretching out before me seemed empty and frightening. *What am I here for? What is the purpose and meaning of it all?*

The questions didn't go away. Even in the middle of a hectic concert tour, I couldn't get them off my mind. I guess you could say I was seeking, though I wouldn't have described it that way at the time. But God knew. And in His love, He has a way of sending His children across the path of a seeking heart.

After one of our concerts, when we were packing up, I spoke with a friendly nineteen-year-old girl who'd stayed around for a while to meet several of us. Right from our first meeting, this girl impressed me. She had none of the prestige or glitter in her life that I thought I had. In fact, she had something I wanted even more. From ten feet away, you could sense the peace and gladness in her heart. It puzzled me. Drew me.

At one point in our conversation, she looked into my eyes and with genuine interest and sincerity asked if I was a Christian. The question caught me so completely off guard that I couldn't fake an answer. After hemming and hawing, I mumbled, "I think so." She sent me to my hotel that night with a booklet that outlined why I was separated from God, how eternity hung in the balance, and how I could know that my sins were forgiven and become a member of God's family.

As I read the little pamphlet, it came to me that some of what I was reading was Scripture. I had never really read the Bible before. My second realization was how far away from those truths and principles my life had drifted. As I read, I felt like a little paper clip being drawn along by a huge magnet. The words in that booklet seemed so right, so pure. Alone in my room, I confessed my sins and invited Jesus into my heart and life. In that moment, of course, I really had no concept of the magnitude of that decision. I was, quite simply, a young girl who had lost her way and now recognized that she was a sinner in need of a Savior. In that quiet moment, God was giving Terry Meeuwsen a "start-over."

Paul writes, "Anyone who belongs to Christ is a new person. The past is forgotten, and everything is new. God has done it all!" (2 Corinthians 5:17–18, CEV). Even as I prayed, a newfound sense of peace washed over me. I slept like a baby that night.

The next day my new friend brought me a modern English translation of the New Testament. In the weeks and months that followed, as I continued to perform in venue after venue with the New Christy Minstrels, I devoured the Word of God. On airplanes, on buses, in restaurants, backstage, and alone in my room at night—I couldn't get enough of it. Where had this been all my life? It was the Word of God that changed my life. Contrary to my former ignorance-based fears, God did not require slavish adherence to unreasonable rules and regulations. For the first time I began to really *know* Him and experience His love and provision for me. I began to realize that His laws were not meant to bind me, but to shelter me.

The more I read and the more time I spent with Him, the more my life changed. Everything was different—I was no longer consumed with myself and my interests. The whole world opened up, and I began to see other people and their needs. Life became a gift and an adventure. It would not be the last time God would mercifully touch my life with a new beginning.

## DEAD END OF A DREAM

A year later, and back home in the Midwest after my tour with the band, I was introduced to a man named Tom Camburn, a successful businessman in Milwaukee, Wisconsin. Tom was thirteen years my senior and the most sophisticated man I had ever met.

As we began to date, I wanted to be perfectly clear

about my standards. I shared with him two personal spiritual determinations I'd made: I would *not* engage in premarital sex, and I would *not* marry someone who wasn't a believer.

Those were certainly excellent standards, and when I set them, I was as sincere as I could be. Sincerity alone, however, will never win the day. Within a year and a half I had abandoned both of them.

Our long-distance relationship became quite serious. We had become intimate with each other, and we were verbally engaged. I rationalized that God would overlook our sexual intimacy because…well, we were in love and *planned* to get married.

When Tom told me that he'd prayed a prayer of commitment to Christ, I took him at his word—even though I saw no evidence of a changed heart or life. I was sure it would all come to pass once we were married. After all, I would be there to encourage him to attend church and find a Bible study group. And of course we would have daily devotions as a couple and pray together.

The truth is, I no longer saw this man the way he was; I saw him the way I *wanted* him to be. After all my travels and empty life in the entertainment world, I was ready for the security of marriage. With willful determination I asked God to bless *my* plans and moved ahead. Even in the first two years of our marriage—when I began to see some alarming cracks in our relationship—I thought if I just stood my ground, loved deeply enough, and prayed hard enough, it would all work out. Learning to surrender my will, my dreams, and my very life to God's will and purposes would be a process for me—and a painful one.

If you had asked me during this time if I was surrendered to the Lord, I would have said yes—and meant it! But in reality, I was still very much in control of my life and my circumstances, expecting that things would work out for me because I was trying so hard and it seemed only fair that they should. Though I loved God sincerely, my life was all about me, and I was still controlling it—all the while sending my laundry list of wants and needs heavenward on a daily basis.

It was in the midst of these chaotic years of marriage that God first began to pry my fingers off of my life. I was desperate to save my marriage, but no matter how hard I tried, the circumstances continued to spiral downward. It was a nightmare...like being in a house slowly sliding down a slope toward destruction. *How could I stop it? What could I do?*

As the worry and turbulence swirled around me,

*The God Adventure*

two of my dearest friends walked alongside me. Linda and Dallas Strom called one night and invited me to a meeting where a messianic Christian named Art Katz was speaking.

I went, aching for a word of direction or encouragement.

That evening Art based his message on Ezekiel 47.

Then the man brought me back to the entrance of the Temple. There I saw a stream flowing eastward from beneath the Temple threshold. This stream then passed to the right of the altar on its south side. The man brought me outside the wall through the north gateway and led me around to the eastern entrance. There I could see the stream flowing out through the south side of the east gateway. Measuring as he went, he led me along the stream for 1,750 feet and told me to go across. At that point the water was up to my ankles. He measured off another 1,750 feet and told me to go across again. This time the water was up to my knees. After another 1,750 feet, it was up to my waist. Then he measured another 1,750 feet, and the river was too deep to cross without swimming.

VV. 1 – 5, NLT

*The River of Life*

He talked about needing to move out of our comfort zones and being willing to let go of what is known and familiar to grab hold of the unknown purposes of God. The very thought of being "out of control" is so uncomfortable—even frightening—for most of us. But God is calling us out into the deep water, where the current of His Holy Spirit guides us, prods us, and moves us along. It's a place where we can't touch bottom and can't be sure what lies around the curve ahead.

It's a daily adventure.

It's a God adventure.

## INTO THE DEEP

When I was a little girl, I used to love to go swimming at the city pool. After splashing and playing in the shallow water, where I could safely stand up, I would wander down to the deep end, where kids were jumping and diving off the diving boards. It looked like they were having so much fun, and I longed to join them—but was much too scared and intimidated to try.

Sometimes my dad would go to the pool with me. When it wasn't crowded, the lifeguards would let him get into the diving well. I would walk out to the end of the diving board, and he would tread water right under the end of the board.

*"Just jump!"* he urged, with a welcoming smile on his face. "I'll be right here with you. Come on—you can do it! You'll float right back up to the top the minute you jump in. And I'm right here waiting for you." I would stand at the end of that diving board with my arms wrapped tightly around myself staring down into that water.

I knew my dad was strong.

I knew he was a good swimmer.

I knew he wouldn't let anything happen to me.

I knew I wasn't going to die.

But I'd never done it before, and *I wouldn't be able to touch the bottom!*

I can't tell you how many times we went through this ritual without my ever jumping. I would climb back down the diving board ladder, filled with frustration and disappointment—and the knowledge that I was missing out on something I really wanted to do.

Finally the day came when my desire to experience the jump into the deep exceeded my fear of the unknown. I came up from that water with my heart pounding, gasping for air. I kicked my feet and stroked frantically till I reached the edge of the pool, and my dad swam with me every inch of the way. I'd done it!

*The River of Life*

I'd really done it! The next couple of jumps still frightened me, but each time got a little easier. Soon I was running and leaping, and in time I began to dive headfirst. But the courage to do it began with the knowledge that my dad was right there with me and would be sure I made it safely through.

When Art Katz spoke that night, he said, "Tonight God is calling us to come out into the river with Him. For some of you, it's the first time you've ever stepped into the current. Maybe tonight you're going to commit to come in up to your ankles. For others of you, God may be calling you to come in up to your knees; for others, it may be up to your waist. But I know there are also some of you here tonight who are being called to come out into the deep…that place where if God isn't more in control than you are, you're not going to make it. I'm going to ask you to stand and make a commitment to the Lord tonight to come into the river, at whatever level you feel called.

"Listen…don't you dare stand up lightly or because you want to look spiritual to the people around you. This is a holy moment, and you'd better enter into it solemnly. Tonight, if you take this step, you'll be telling God, 'Whatever it takes, whatever You want, Lord—I will do it!'"

Art asked those who wanted to come into the river

*The God Adventure*

up to their ankles to stand. There was a holy hush as different ones across the auditorium rose slowly to their feet. I sat with my face buried in my hands as he invited people to commit to coming in up to their knees, and then waists. I could hear my heavenly Father's voice. *"Come out into the deep with Me, My daughter. It's time to let go and trust Me with all of your life."*

When that final invitation came, I stood up, trembling, tears streaming down my face. I was afraid of what the cost might be, but I was even more afraid to say no. I knew I had reached a point of no return. I told the Lord that I no longer wanted to live in a safe, predictable place of commitment. I wanted to live abandoned to His purposes in the current of His Spirit. My life needed to be shaped by my relationship with God. My focus needed to be on growing closer to Him, no matter what happened to my marriage.

The commitment that night began a God adventure that would shape the rest of my life.

I could no longer touch bottom. And that was okay, because my Father was swimming with me every inch of the way.

# The Hard Trail of New Beginnings

*He has delivered us from such a deadly peril,*
*and he will deliver us. On him we have set our*
*hope that he will continue to deliver us.*

2 CORINTHIANS 1:10

3

THE DEATH of my marriage was slow and painful.

It began with a realization that my husband had a serious drinking problem. I went to Alcoholics Anonymous (AA), hoping he would join me. I found some encouragement and help for myself in these meetings, but...nothing else changed.

It would be several years before I was able to face his infidelity. Even then, I hoped we could still (somehow) "work it out." Tom was gone almost all the time—I had no idea where. When I went to church on Sundays, he would come home for a fresh change of clothes. I began to see a Christian counselor, and Tom initially agreed to come with me. And he did...twice. Then never showed up again.

One day I called him at work and asked him to please come home and talk to me. When he arrived, I poured my heart out to him, begging him to come back and work on our marriage. At that moment, Tom did what was probably the kindest thing he'd ever

*The God Adventure*

done for me. He said, "You know, I figured you were going to ask me this, and I've done a lot of thinking about it. I've decided I'm not the kind of person who should be married!"

I was devastated. I soon found out my husband was living with an eighteen-year-old bartender. A short time later, he moved to Las Vegas and ran gambling junkets to and from the casinos there. When I realized he wasn't coming back, I filed for divorce.

I had married expecting it to last forever. Five years later, alone in a courtroom with my attorney and a judge I didn't know, eight years of my life were blotted out with the pound of a gavel. Failure, disillusionment, and confusion weighed heavily on my heart.

I had tried everything I knew to keep my marriage alive. What do you do when your best isn't good enough? I fasted, prayed, went through counseling, bargained with God, wept, and pleaded for His mercy.

And God was there. He wasn't giving me what I pleaded for, He wasn't pulling me out of my problems and heartaches, but He walked with me through the middle of them.

*When I thought I couldn't bear another day—another hour—of heartache, He would renew my strength and carry me through my circumstances.*

*When the sense of failure seemed overwhelming, He would wrap Himself around me and cover my shame.*

*When the death of my dreams threatened to swallow me in grief, He would hold me and whisper promises from His Word into my broken heart.*

In later years, I've reflected on the truth of His Word in the Beatitudes: "Blessed are those who mourn, for they will be comforted" (Matthew 5:4). When our needs are crushing, when our situation is desperate, when our wounds are profound, when our hearts are empty and desolate, His comfort reaches deeper places than it has ever reached before. As Paul wrote in one of the darkest moments of his life, "For just as the sufferings of Christ flow over into our lives, so also through Christ our comfort overflows" (2 Corinthians 1:5).

I wanted resurrection in this marriage—life out of death. But He called me to a place of deeper surrender. Most often I didn't understand the "why" of what was happening, but I always knew He was with me.

A deep sadness enveloped me at that time. I felt like the sun would never shine again in quite the same way, and I would never feel that kind of joy that simply fills you with a sense of the overwhelming beauty of life. I saw it all from outside myself, but couldn't seem to take it in.

Months went by under a cloud of slate gray.

And then one morning everything changed.

I walked outside and the air was filled with the fresh smell of the earth warming in the spring sunshine. I could see new buds on the trees and jonquils peeking up through the thawing snow. I closed my eyes and breathed in the sheer beauty of it all. Grief, like a veil, seemed to slip from my shoulders. Hope, like the shy, tentative fingers of dawn, began to seep into my heart.

Just that quickly, on that fragrant spring morning, I felt as though I had emerged from the shadows into a new beginning. God adventures lay ahead of me, like the prospect of high vistas on a mountain trail you've never walked before.

The fact is, new God adventures frequently emerge from the ruins of great disappointments and sorrows. When life moves along smoothly, when our routines are comfortable, when we find ourselves in a nice, easy, autopilot mode of living, adventuring with God rarely enters our mind. Why rock the boat? Why climb out from under the warm covers of familiarity and security?

Heavy trials or loss, however, rearrange our world, stripping away our sense of assurance and ease. We cling to God with everything we have in us; we stretch out full length on His provision; we cry out for His wisdom and direction. And when the temporary paralysis of grief finally begins to lift from our soul, when the illusion of security has been thoroughly shattered and scattered to the winds, we look around at our world through new eyes. And though our wounds have only begun to heal, we find ourselves open to the whisper of God's Spirit, calling us to new ventures, new dreams.

No one wants the pain. No one wants the grief or loss. No one wants the confusion or that sickening sense that life is coming unraveled. Yet those uncomfortable, sometimes devastating situations in our lives become the very trailhead for a new and closer walk with Jesus.

## THE ADVENT OF ANDY

Despite this new sense of aliveness, I had no desire *at all* to get into another relationship. I had dated Tom for three years and been married to him for five, so being single again was very foreign and I felt painfully vulnerable. The very thought of dating again made me nauseated.

I was working in television in Milwaukee, Wisconsin, at the time, and I threw myself into my work. It was a necessary time of personal reflection and spiritual evaluation. I continued to see a counselor, wanting to understand why I'd made the choices I did in my relationship with Tom. I needed to know that I wouldn't rationalize and make the same mistakes again. I didn't trust *myself* anymore, much less trust a man.

Andy Friedrich showed up at a retirement party for a departing fellow employee. The TV station I worked for also housed AM and FM radio stations. I knew little about radio and even less about who worked for these stations. Andy was a salesman for the AM station.

After putting in an appearance and congratulating the retiring engineer, I headed back to my office to pack up for the day. As I walked out of the gathering, I felt a tap on my shoulder.

"Excuse me—you're a Christian, aren't you?"

A tall, sandy-haired man stood in my path. "Yes, I am." Who was this guy? I had no idea.

"Well, I am, too," he continued, "but I have a lot of questions. Would you be willing to go to lunch one day and talk about it?"

*Lunch?* I thought. *I don't even know you. I don't want to go to lunch.* But in that moment I felt backed into a corner. "Uh, sure...I guess so."

"Great! Thanks!" He moved back into the crowd. Irritated, I walked down the hall to my office, where a couple of my coworkers were finishing up the day's scheduling. "I cannot believe what just happened!" I told them. "I just told some guy I don't even know that I'd have lunch with him. He totally caught me off guard, and I couldn't think of an excuse." I was *not* happy!

"What does he look like?" my friends asked. When I described him, someone said, "Oh, that's Andy Friedrich. He works for WTMJ radio." I was determined to get myself out of this lunch thing.

Months went by, and the legal proceedings for divorce moved on relentlessly. Sometimes it felt like I was walking a road six inches deep in mud, and I could hardly lift my feet. I was so afraid of being swallowed up by the whole process—of being pulled back into the past and reliving all those old, depressive emotions. In spite of my fears, however, God kept me moving forward, step by labored step.

And this Andy person? Well, weeks went by and I didn't see him. Truthfully, I had forgotten the whole incident.

Five months later I had gone into work early to take care of some last-minute meeting preparation. Suddenly there he was, standing in the doorway.

"Well," he smiled, "I'm back."

"Oh?" I replied. "Were you gone?"

"Wow! You really know how to hurt a guy!"

There it was again. That tone of friendly familiarity that so irritated me. How did this guy keep popping up? Why was he bothering me? What nerve he had! He told me that he had left the company for a position somewhere else and was now working for WTMJ again.

"Listen," he said, "I'd still like to have that lunch, if you're willing. And, by the way, I heard that you're getting divorced and I want you to know that's *not* why I'm asking you to lunch."

Once again, Andy's directness took me right out of my game plan. Why did this man always seem to throw me into such confusion? I wanted to say no and not have to deal with this, but I didn't know how to do that...graciously.

"All right," I heard myself saying. "Lunch will be fine." *But only once,* I added to myself.

I deliberately sandwiched that lunch between other appointments, comforting myself with the security of a sure escape hatch. Talking to Andy, however...really wasn't so bad. The conversation was easygoing and comfortable. He genuinely wanted to know about my faith and had questions that had been plaguing him for months. A friend had led him to the Lord several years before but hadn't been around to disciple him in any way. He'd been given a Bible, but he really didn't know where to start or how to study it. Inherently, Andy knew that being a Christian should mean some kind of a change was necessary in his lifestyle and his choices, but he didn't know how to go about making that happen.

Our conversation went nonstop, and before I knew it, our lunchtime was up. *Would I be willing to get together again?* he wanted to know. Inexplicably, I agreed to lunch the following week. I figured a crowded restaurant was a safe place to be. Once again we talked about issues of faith and shared our own individual backgrounds and upbringing.

On the way back to the station, Andy asked me if I was dating.

"No!" I said.

"When will you begin to date?"

"I really have no idea."

"Will you let me know?"

"Probably not."

"Well, I guess I'll just have to keep checking then, won't I?"

Boy, I hoped this guy wasn't going to end up being a pain. I headed for my office and immersed myself in paperwork.

## DRIVING LESSONS

Within days, I received word from my husband's former company that I needed to turn in his company car. Tom had lost his job and moved to Las Vegas, but I was still driving his company car—our last vestige of shared property. I had just bought my own house, and now—somehow—I was going to have to buy a car as well.

One more thing! I was starting to feel overwhelmed. In a conversation with my brother, he suggested I buy a stick shift because it was more economical. There was just one problem: I'd never driven a stick in my whole life. And (wouldn't you know it?) the only person I knew who drove a stick shift was Andy Friedrich. That gorgeous cranberry-red sports car.

I decided to ask him if I could drive it around a parking lot to see if I felt like I could master it. He agreed (with a smile) and asked if I wanted to get a burger afterward. Since he was nice enough to let me drive his car, I didn't feel like I could say no.

When he picked me up and we got in the car to head for a vacant parking lot, he said, "Can I ask you a question?"

"Sure," I said.

"Is this our first date? 'Cause if it is, I don't want to miss it!"

Good night, he'd cornered me again! I grudgingly conceded that I supposed this was a first date. And though I was very self-conscious and frequently uncomfortable, we did have a lovely evening. And I ended up buying a stick shift.

Andy and I dated for a year before we married. I was trying to figure out who I was and to learn to trust again. He waited patiently. In the pain of my divorce and the overwhelming sense of aloneness, I had come to know the Lord in a new and deeper way. It's amazing how God can make something positive out of loss and pain. I was determined not to lose the ground I'd gained spiritually. No matter how much I loved Andy, my relationship with the Lord would always be number one. I knew obedience was the gauge of where I was with God. And as our relationship deepened, God tested my resolve.

My best friends, Linda and Dallas, were in full-time ministry and Andy and I spent a lot of time with them. We talked constantly about God's Word, His faithfulness, and the challenges of living a life of faith.

After one such conversation, I could tell that Andy had become extremely frustrated. "I feel so out of it when I'm with you and your friends. You're all quoting

Scripture verses and talking about stuff I don't understand. I just don't feel like I fit in—and I don't know how to get to where you are. You've been a Christian for so much longer than me. I just don't think I can do this."

Andy's feelings took me by surprise. I felt a sense of alarm. By now, we had begun to really care about each other. What should I do? Everything had seemed to be going so well. Was I going to lose the man in my life so soon after finding him? *Should I scale back on meeting with strong believers and talking about things of the Lord?*

I knew in my heart that I couldn't do that. If I changed my activities and focus to things *he* was more comfortable with, I would be moving away from where God had me and the accountability and support I had as a believer. On the other hand, if I didn't accommodate his discomfort, I could lose him.

I felt sick inside, but knew what I had to do. "Andy," I told him, "I can't come to where you are. You have to decide whether or not you can or want to come to where I am." When we said good-bye, I really didn't know if I would see Andy again.

I felt like God brought me to a place where I had to put my relationship with Andy on the altar. God was first in my life, and I had already learned the painful lessons of going my own way, merely paying lip service to Him. As difficult as it was, I knew I really had no choice. I cried myself to sleep that night.

Several days later, Andy called and we began to see each other again. He got into the Word, we attended Bible studies together, and he grew in the Lord. Soon Linda and Dallas were leading us through a six-month premarital biblical counseling program. On June 6, 1981, in a small, quiet ceremony, Dallas married us.

And a new adventure began.


## OUT OF OUR COMFORT ZONES

Early on in our dating, Andy and I had begun to pray together. We had made a commitment to God and to each other that we wanted to be "risk-takers" for the Lord. We told God we did not want to walk in safe, predictable paths. We wanted to be willing to live outside our comfort zone if it suited His purposes.

Watch out when you pray such a prayer! God will take you seriously. As sincere as we were, we had no idea what we were committing to. And that was okay. God knew we were sincere, and *we* knew He wouldn't call us to anything He wouldn't equip us for. I am, however, very glad we couldn't see all that was ahead.

It wasn't long before God took us up on that "risk-taker" prayer. When Andy and I married, we had no intention of leaving Milwaukee. Within three months, we were living in Virginia Beach, Virginia, where Andy worked for WTAR-radio and I hosted an early-morning TV show called *USam*, a creation of the Christian Broadcasting Network (CBN). Though we both ached with the loss of family and friends back home, it was a God adventure that took us away from two very busy lives and gave us a year to really focus on each other. I had no idea that my work that year with CBN would bring me back to Virginia Beach twelve years later.

I hosted *USam* for one year before CBN decided to cancel the show. Andy and I headed back to Milwaukee, Wisconsin, with hopes of starting a family. I went back to work for WTMJ, the NBC affiliate, doing documentaries and specials. Almost immediately I became pregnant. Our son Drew was born in August of 1983. I was thirty-four years old.

Adoption had always been something I wanted to do. I can't explain why. It's almost as though God put that desire within me. When Drew turned one, we spent the morning at the adoption agency and threw his birthday party in the afternoon. We applied for an older child and were matched with a five-and-a-half-year-old little

*The Hard Trail of New Beginnings*

boy from Korea. We were thrilled and began preparing for his arrival.

A couple of months went by and he still had not come. At about the same time, I discovered I was pregnant again…and that our adoption effort had fallen through. In July of 1985, our daughter Tory was born. When she turned one, we spent the morning at the adoption agency and threw her party in the afternoon. This time we processed in for a Korean infant. Nine months later we received a picture and bio of the most precious baby boy. We were elated. Joseph Philip (J. P.) arrived four months later, and I felt like all my dreams had come true. God had blessed me beyond my wildest hopes.

Whenever Andy and I talked about our family, we would privately say to each other that in a perfect world we would love to have four children. If we'd had an opportunity to adopt again, we would have adopted a black or biracial child. We felt so blessed, however, that we never even thought to pray about it.

One evening as we were all sitting around the dinner table, the phone rang. It was an old friend who had moved to Oklahoma to go to Bible school. The daughter of the family she was staying with had been dating a football player at the University and just found out she was pregnant. To our amazement our friend called to ask if we would be interested in adopting a biracial baby. We were astonished that God would give us the desire of our hearts without our even asking Him. We were actually in the delivery room when our son Tyler was born. He was beautiful. We headed back to Wisconsin totally content with our four precious and unique children.

I had just turned forty and Andy was forty-three.

The next few years held numerous challenges... building a home, job changes, starting a business, and weathering a financial crisis, to name a few. The one constant in our lives was the blessing of family and friends. In Milwaukee, we lived right in between both sets of grandparents—less than two hours from each. We had many wonderful Christian friends and hosted a large Bible study in our home.

Over the years, I'd been flying down to Virginia Beach to fill in on *The 700 Club* when their cohosts would go on vacation or when CBN was looking for a new cohost. I had no intention of taking a permanent position there. One day, out of the blue, *The 700 Club* called me and said that Sheila Walsh, who had cohosted for five years, was leaving. Would I be interested in moving to Virginia and taking the position of cohost?

That was easy to answer. *No!*

I had left work shortly after J. P. arrived and had no desire to go back. Leave our families? Our friends? Our church? God couldn't possibly be in this! A friend suggested I pray about it. (Novel idea!) I had no problem doing that because I was *sure* God would never ask me to leave family and home.

When Andy and I began to pray, asking God to show us His will, I began to feel a strange uneasiness within me. I couldn't even contemplate telling Andy's parents or mine that we were even considering such a long-distance move. At the weekly Bible study in our home, we had been asking God to send forth believers from our midst to go into the world to share the message of His love.

But not *us*! Surely not us, Lord! I wouldn't let myself think about it.

Finally, CBN needed an answer. We prayed in earnest, asking God to clearly show us, confirm it, and give us peace if we were to go. Deep down, I knew very well what God was saying, but I was heartsick. I'd like to be able to tell you that I packed up our belongings while whistling a happy tune with a sense of adventure in my heart. The truth is, I cried at the drop of a hat just thinking about leaving. My best friend, Linda, and I couldn't look at each other without getting teary.

We were moving ahead in obedience, but my heart wasn't cooperating. I was learning an important lesson. When you choose to step out of your comfort zone in obedience to God's leading, He will meet you as you move into His purposes.

That's the thing about God adventures. His grace and enabling comes in the moment of need...and sometimes not one minute sooner. Oh, and one other thing. Often a God adventure comes when you least expect it. Ten years after we'd come back to CBN, when many of our friends were becoming empty nesters, God whispered an invitation into our hearts that took our breath away. It has turned our lives upside down—and I wouldn't have wanted to miss a second of it!

# When Adventure Comes Knocking

"Have I not commanded you? Be strong and courageous.
Do not be terrified; do not be discouraged,
for the LORD your God will
be with you wherever you go."

JOSHUA 1:9

4

I SAT very still as my husband and I drove the twenty miles to pick up our sixteen-year-old daughter from a friend's house.

How could I say this to Andy? How could I explain? What would he think?

Since I couldn't think of how to start the conversation, I decided to just plunge in and leave the results to God.

"Andy," I said, "there's something I need to talk to you about."

He shot me a quick, concerned glance. Those can be scary words coming from a wife. "Okay," he said.

"Could I just share my heart with you on this—from beginning to end—and not have you say anything until I get to the end of it?"

Now he was even more concerned. "All right," he said. "Shoot."

"First of all, I want to tell that I'm not looking for a 'yes' here, okay?"

*The God Adventure*

He nodded carefully, keeping his eyes on the road.

"What I'm looking for," I went on, "is some sort of sanity in the midst of a very insane idea."

I can assure you that in that moment I had my husband's full attention. And I needed it! I felt we might be on the verge—the very cusp—of a God adventure like we'd never experienced before, and it was a fearful thing. But in spite of myself, I couldn't deny a feeling of growing excitement underneath. Something was happening. Something big. And I had a strong hunch that God was in it.

It all began in a routine sort of way—routine in the sense that it was one television interview in a line of many, many such interviews. After all, that's what I do. I host several different programs at CBN, the Christian Broadcasting Network in Virginia Beach, Virginia, and regularly conduct on-camera interviews.

On a program called *Living the Life,* I sat down with Nancy Hathaway, a woman from nearby Williamsburg. It was your somewhat-typical human interest story, and as I prepped for our interview I had no concept at all how that forty-minute session would change my life.

That's the way it is with God adventures. They slip covertly into ordinary days as you go about doing ordinary tasks. And suddenly in the midst of the common, average, workaday realities of life, you find yourself confronted by that which is not ordinary at all.

Remember Gideon? He was threshing wheat while hiding from the Midianites in a wine press. It was something he'd probably done for a long, long time. You might say it was routine. But then "the angel of the LORD came and sat down under an oak" nearby, and said, "The LORD is with you, mighty warrior." *Mighty warrior?* He was hiding from the enemy! But God had an adventure for Gideon that would change his identity. Gideon said, "Yes," and nothing was ever routine for him again (see Judges 6–8).

Nancy and her husband, Steve, were in their late forties. It was a second marriage for both, and they had no children of their own, although Nancy had a grown son by her previous marriage. And even though it was rather late in life to be considering such a thing, they had decided they wanted to adopt an orphaned child from another country. Granted, this was normally a time when couples begin to look forward to an easier life—travel, recreation, hobbies, and so on. This couple, however, came to the conclusion that they could either retire early and live comfortably adjacent to some golf course…or they could change a life by adopting an older child from a needy country.

They opted for adoption. Nancy had been on some

mission trips to Ukraine and spoke a little Russian, so that was the place they decided to begin their search for an orphaned girl.

The more Nancy talked, the less this seemed a "typical interview" for me. I was moved by their reasoning and their decision to take a step like this. After the program was over, I asked her if she would be willing to come back with their little girl once they brought her home so we could do a follow-up program. Nancy said, "Fine," and that was that. For the time being.

During this time, I was reading Bruce Wilkinson's book *The Prayer of Jabez*. I felt a desire to begin to ask God, as Jabez had, to "expand my territory! Let your hand be with me, and keep me from evil…." I was not asking for material blessings. I wanted Him to use me more. At the same time, I'd been reading about prayer and fasting. One author, Lou Engle, described fasting as "exchanging the temporary pleasure of food for the extravagant pleasure of more of Him." I was so taken with that statement. A fresh desire rose in my heart to pray for my four children—for the quality of their walk with the Lord and that He would get their attention in a world of a thousand competing loyalties.

I was in the middle of that fast for my children when Nancy and Steve came back from Ukraine with their new nine-year-old daughter, Natalie.

As we prepared to go on the air, we had our usual production meeting. I remember saying to our producer, "Boy, I can't wait to meet them and talk to them about this process." Our sons J. P. and Tyler were adopted, but they came to us as infants. And I just couldn't imagine what it would be like to go to an orphanage and adopt an older child. What would you do…line them up along the wall, look them up and down and compare them? Wait for one of them to stand out somehow—for some shaft of heavenly light to beam through a dusty window and illuminate one? How would you do it? What about those not "chosen"? It was a great mystery to me.

Steve and Nancy had gone to Ukraine with the intention of adopting only one child, but they had the capacity to bring back two. That's the way it is when you adopt internationally; they do that in case you find a sibling you weren't expecting.

When they arrived at the orphanage, the director said, "I have three sisters I want you to look at."

"Oh," Steve replied, "we came here to adopt one child. And we only have approval for two. We can't do three."

"Wait just a minute, please," the director said. And she left the room.

She came back a few minutes later and said, "It will be all right. The oldest sister said she would stay behind so the younger two can have a chance to live in America."

As the producer related the story, everyone in the meeting was just stunned. All of us were moved to tears. *What kind of child sacrifices herself for the sake of her younger siblings? What must have been going on in the hearts of those children as they waited for the Hathaways' decision?* Steve and Nancy had no desire to break up the sisters, so they ended up adopting one child, little Natalie, as they had set out to do.

Later, as I continued my fast, I was in the throes of praying for my own children. But suddenly I found myself praying intensely for the three Ukrainian girls. I poured out my heart to the Lord, praying that He would find a family for them—that somehow they would be allowed to remain together.

As the days went by, I began waking up in the night thinking about those girls. And time and again, my thoughts would drift toward them during the day. I ached for them. It just broke my heart to think that they had lost their parents and then might lose each other!

One day, as I was fasting and praying for my own four kids, the Lord spoke to me and said, "What is the fast that I require of you, but that you take care of widows and orphans?"

Now what did He mean by that? He couldn't be talking to *me* about those girls…could He? I already had four kids. And I was fifty-three at the time. Way too old to consider adding to our family like that. Ridiculous thought!

I chalked up that strong impression to a hormone overload—or job stress—or…something else.

But I just couldn't get those girls off my mind. I enlisted two friends to pray with me for two weeks asking God to clarify what He was laying on my heart.

And that's how I came to the conversation with my husband in the car, as we drove those twenty miles to pick up our daughter.

"Andy," I said, "am I just crazy to even think about this? What are your thoughts? How do you feel about it?"

"Terry, have you thought about how old we'll be when these girls graduate from high school?"

"No, I guess not. And I really don't know anything about them. I don't know their ages; I don't know their names; I don't know why they're in the orphanage."

Andy sighed. "Well," he said, "I guess that's one way we could ask God to give us a sign. If we're not too old to do this, maybe we're supposed to pursue it and try to keep those girls together."

So that was our agreement. That we would move ahead on this, and if God gave us green lights we would continue. And if He didn't want us to do it, He was certainly able to select from about a million different roadblocks to barricade our path.

This seems to me a likely way for a God adventure to begin. First there was strong interest—something that really captured my heart. Then I found myself moved to pray regarding that interest. Sometime later I was seeking God through prayer and fasting, before His throne, my heart wide open, pleading for my children. And in those moments, the Holy Spirit spoke to me about something I hadn't really considered before.

Our direction seemed confirmed as I talked it over with my husband. And we agreed to be open to the idea. To go forward in obedience, waiting on God to stop us or redirect us.

What if I hadn't fasted or been praying so intently? Would the adventure still have come our way? Maybe. But I'm not sure I would have had the right heart attitude needed to hear and obey.

I can't help but recall how one of the first extended God adventures in the book of Acts—Paul's first missionary journey—began:

While they were ministering to the Lord and
fasting, the Holy Spirit said, "Set apart for Me
Barnabas and Saul for the work to which I
have called them." Then, when they had fasted
and prayed and laid their hands on them, they
sent them away.

ACTS 13:2−3, NASB

Was this crazy idea of adopting three girls at one
time really an "adventure" sent from God? Was this
what He wanted for us? Would it be too much for us?
Surely God didn't want to overwhelm us.

We kept praying. And we kept talking.

"How are we going to pay for this?" Andy asked
me, as we talked later that night.

"Well," I replied, "I've thought about that, too. The
only way I know how we could afford this is to take
money out of our retirement fund. I know—we don't
have a lot in there, but we do have some. I guess I just
keep thinking about standing before Jesus someday
and having to admit that because of protecting ourselves and protecting our comfort, these little girls
would be separated for the rest of their lives. What
would we say to Him?"

Neither of us had an answer for that.

"But what about our age, Terry? Don't you see that as a disadvantage?"

"Yes. But—how would I feel if I were one of those girls? Would I rather have a nice home, brothers and sisters, a hope and a future, and parents who are a bit older than everybody else's....or would I rather grow up in an orphanage all my life?"

Both of us knew that was a no-brainer. If the girls had a chance, we knew they would want to come. We went to bed that night with no details at all—and with no idea how this could happen or how we could manage it. We just knew we wanted to be obedient, and we wanted to be open to God's will, no matter where it led.

And those are the two prerequisites to a God adventure.

# When the Vision Tarries

A man's heart plans his way,
But the LORD directs his steps.

PROVERBS 16:9, NKJV

5

THERE'S SOMETHING that happens once you have sensed God's purpose and have done your best to step out in obedience and follow it…even if they're baby steps.

It's difficult to describe. You might call it an initial confirmation. It's that wind-at-your-back kind of feeling that you're really on the right road, heading in the right direction. Andy and I began to feel like the girls already belonged to us. But it was time to bring the rest of the family on board. It was time to sit down with our four kids and lay out the adventure before them.

Frankly, I had no idea how they were going to feel about it. The idea of increasing the family from six to nine in one fell swoop would take a little getting used to. And it would obviously mean that everyone would have a smaller slice of Mom and Dad.

We had agreed that if the kids were opposed to launching out on this venture, that would be the end of it. We would not try to push through a red light as significant as that one.

So we called a family powwow one night in the living room and began telling them the story of the three orphan girls in faraway Ukraine. As Andy and I shared, I don't think the kids had a clue where we were going with the story. I could see it in their eyes; they thought we were going to wrap it up by saying, "So let's tithe some of our allowance and see if we can help them."

And then we dropped the bomb.

"Kids...we think we're supposed to adopt these three girls. Make them part of the family. And we want to know how you feel about that."

Four stunned faces looked across the room at us. Suddenly, my sixteen-year-old daughter, Tory, began to cry. My heart sank in that moment. Tory loved being the only girl and was very close to me. I moved over next to her, put my arm around her shoulders, and said, "Why are you crying, Tory?"

"I don't know," she said. And she cried and cried.

"Tory," I said gently, "do you think I'm going to love you any less because there would be more girls in our family? That's not possible, you know. I know doing this might change our times together—things might not be the same—but we'll always have each other, and we'll always have a special relationship."

As Tory gently sobbed, I looked around at the boys—Tyler, Drew, and J. P. "I just want you all to know that we're not committed to do anything yet. We care very much what you think. This is your family, too, and you have the option of saying no to this."

Tory looked up at Andy and me through her tears. "I know that all the things I'm crying about are selfish reasons. I know what you're wanting to do is the right thing, so—so just let me cry and go ahead and do what you need to do."

The boys were much more accepting of the idea right from the start. Typical males, they were more concerned about logistics: Who was going to sleep in what bedroom. Drew, our oldest, said, "I'm going off to college this fall, so I'm not going to be here anyway. My room's available, so go for it!"

Tory wondered if she could keep her own bedroom, and we assured her that she could. And then she looked up with a little smile. "Can I go with you to get the girls?"

Immediately, in that moment, I knew it was the right thing. I knew that if we adopted the girls, Tory needed to travel to Ukraine with us. I felt sure that taking her was going to be part of God's work in her heart, helping her bond to the girls and make space for them in her world.

*The God Adventure*

Next up for Andy and me was telling our parents, brothers, and sisters about our intention. Here's what we did. On a previous trip to Ukraine, I'd purchased a bunch of those stacking *matrioshka* or "nesting" dolls. So we made some little adoption announcements, tucked each one in with a set of the dolls, wrapped them up in little packages, and sent them off to the family members, hoping they would all get them at close to the same time.

Our families were wonderful. They prayed with us. They affirmed us. They stood with us. And if they thought we were crazy or had gone off the deep end, they were kind enough not to tell us so!

## "STOP US IF YOU WANT TO, LORD!"

When you launch out on a God adventure like this, the implications don't hit you all at once. Sometimes, they catch up with you down the road a ways. Yes, you've reminded yourself again and again how this will change your life, change your family—but you haven't really thought through all the many, many particulars.

It had begun to dawn on Andy and me that if we followed through on this, there would probably *never* be a time in our lives when we could cut back, kick back, and relax a little more, as many people do in their later years. We gulped at the probable financial challenges. We were not only throwing ourselves seven years back in the parenting process; we were also taking on three little human beings who would most certainly have emotional baggage. Many, many needs would be uncovered layer by layer as time went by.

Andy and I would need to speak into those deep needs and hurts with the Word of God, and with wisdom from the Spirit of God. We would need to pray for our family as never before—not only for emotional healing, but for spiritual protection for all of us. When we thought about these things, there were times when we felt frightened and overwhelmed. We were very aware of how inadequate we were to meet such needs. And then God would remind us that we were never adequate in our own strength to begin with! We don't have what it takes to be loving spouses and parents and people who are involved in so many aspects of the Lord's work. If He could meet us in our needs and be our adequacy now, He would certainly be adequate for us tomorrow...and tomorrow and tomorrow.

Along the way, we kept praying, "Lord, if we're not supposed to do this, if we're heading in a wrong direction, please show us. Give us a red light and don't let us go any further." Truthfully, there was a part of us that

*The God Adventure*

really hoped we *would* get a red light so we could go on with life—safe and footloose and fancy-free. We could forget about contemplating all those scary implications of adopting three young Ukrainian girls and go back to life as it was. Nicely busy and comfortably familiar.

In the meantime, we began to move things around in our house and make plans for who-would-sleep-where. Yes, our son was going off to college, and we would need his room in the new equation. But at the same time, we didn't want him to feel like he was being pushed out of the family—or that he couldn't come back.

It was going to be a challenge to make sure that everybody felt loved, valued, and taken care of.

## When the Vision Tarries

Most always, your God adventure will be tested. There will come a point when an "impossible obstacle" looms up in your path, and you will begin to wonder if you heard God right in the first place.

Many God adventures fail right here, at this crucial point, when the vision seems in danger of dying, and all your plans seem to be collapsing like a house of cards.

That moment came for us with an e-mail from our

facilitator in Kiev. "We've got some bad news for you from the National Adoption Center," it began. "The girls' paperwork cannot be found. We don't know if it was lost or if it was never done, or what happened, but it's not to be found at the NAC in any of the files. We have no choice but to redo everything. And by Ukrainian law, once that paperwork is processed from the local level through the regional level and then on to Kiev, there's a one-year waiting period before the girls can be adopted."

The problem was, *our* paperwork *had* been completed and was in the process of being finalized. Once that happened, the clock started ticking on a one-year time limit. After that deadline had passed, all of that paperwork and all of the thousands of dollars spent getting to that point would be down the drain. And the girls—*our* girls—were stuck in that orphanage, for at least another year.

I remember standing in the bedroom we'd prepared for the girls, and my heart just cried out, *God, are they ever going to live here? Are they ever going to sleep in these beds? Or was this just an effort in futility, and You're teaching us something totally unrelated to this?*

I felt like the Lord spoke to my heart in that moment and said, "Hold on to the vision, for though it tarry, it will surely come to pass."

It sounded like something from the Bible. But it was no verse I could remember reading or learning. I didn't know if it was Scripture or not; I just knew it was something the Lord whispered to me in my moment of distress and desolation.

The next day I came into work and said to my assistant, "Rhonda, will you look up this sentence and see if it comes from the Word while I'm on the program today? I need to know if this is from the Bible or not."

When I came out of the program, Rhonda was standing in the hall, smiling. "It *is* from Scripture," she said. "It's very close to what God told the prophet in Habakkuk 2:3. Listen to this!"

"For the vision is yet for the appointed time;
    It hastens toward the goal and it will not fail.
Though it tarries, wait for it;
    For it will certainly come, it will not delay."

N A S B

A surge of joy welled up in my heart. I felt like God had sent me a specific word of encouragement through His Word. *Wait for the vision. Hang on to the vision.* I needed to stand on that word. I needed to keep my grip on the vision God had given me and say,

"This will come to pass because God ordained it."

A few days later, an e-mail confirmed what I already knew would happen. "It's a miracle. The paperwork has been found. The girls are available. Come as soon as possible."

## THE DAY ARRIVES

The day finally came when we got into a car in Kiev, Ukraine, and began the twelve-hour drive to Berdyansk, and the orphanage.

We were very nervous. It was one thing to love these girls from afar and to feel like they were ours, but it was quite another thing to think of them suddenly walking into the room with you. Would they like us? Would they think we were too old? Would they want to leave Ukraine? How would they feel about coming to America?

We had no idea what to expect, but then…we were pulling into the driveway…getting out of the car…walking up the walk…stepping inside. The orphanage director met us in her office. We would need more paperwork before we could take the girls, she told us, but we would be allowed to see them.

The time had come.

*The God Adventure*

I remembered the words from Habakkuk: *"For the vision is yet for the appointed time; it hastens toward the goal and it will not fail. Though it tarries, wait for it; for it will certainly come, it will not delay."*

The night before in the hotel, my husband Andy and I were in bed, and he said, "Have you thought about what it will be like tomorrow? I mean, what are we going to do when they walk into the room?"

"You mean, do we hug them?"

"That's exactly what I mean. What do you think they're expecting?"

"I don't think we can plan it. I think we have to just go and let God orchestrate the whole thing."

Through a translator, the director said, "The girls have been waiting. They're very excited."

Out of the corner of my eye I saw a room across the hallway and three little faces peeking out a window, trying to get a glimpse of us. My heart was pounding...but the director wasn't through asking questions yet.

"How do you know that you'll love the girls?" she asked.

"I just know that we will," I told her. "We've loved them from the first time we heard anything about them." And by this time we knew their names. Alysa was the oldest—thirteen at the time. Zoya, eleven, was next, and nine-year-old Sophia was the youngest.

"What if you get them to America and there are difficult times?" she persisted.

"Difficult times?" I said. "That could happen with the children we have in the family right now! Nobody has any guarantees. We don't love them because they behave well—we love them because they're ours in our hearts."

"Well," she said (at last), "I'm going to bring them in for you to meet."

She left the room, and a few seconds later the door flew open and three little girls ran right into our arms. *"Mama! Papa!"* they said. They hugged us and hugged their new big sister. "We love you," we said to them, and with shining eyes and halting English they said, "We love you."

The vision had tarried. We waited and waited for it. And at God's appointed time, it came. All the sweeter for waiting.

# An Adventure That Tells a Story

Consider the incredible love that the Father
has shown us in allowing us to be called
"children of God"—and that is not just
what we are called, but what we ARE.

1 JOHN 3:1, PHILLIPS

6

ONCE UPON A TIME...on a small peninsula jutting
from a semiarid plain on the northern coast of the Sea
of Azov, in the city of Berdyansk in southeastern
Ukraine, something wonderful was about to happen to
three little orphaned sisters.

And they didn't know a thing about it.

Alysa, Zoya, and Sophia lived in a small, nonde-
script, rather sterile orphanage in an old neighborhood
in the northern part of the city. As the three sisters
walked through their routine days, thinking mostly
routine thoughts, they had no concept or awareness of
the Something Wonderful just around the corner. In
the gray light of dawn, they got out of their beds in the
dormitory, washed their faces and brushed their hair,
dressed themselves for the day in their secondhand
orphanage clothes, ate the usual breakfast at the long
tables in the dining room, and went off to their lessons.

They had each other, which was a comfort, but

*The God Adventure*

they had no real hope of life being much different than it was. Everything was just like always.

Or so they thought.

But it really wasn't.

*If only they had known.* If only they'd had some inkling that someone—several someones—in impossibly-far-away America lay awake at night thinking about them. And not only thinking, but praying for them, longing for them, shedding tears for them, and working very hard to change their lives forever. What an incredible thought that would have been for them. They might have walked along those long, gray-tiled hallways with a little extra bounce in their step. What a difference it would have made in their lives!

The three sisters may have felt abandoned and alone. They may have sighed as they slipped under their covers at night and thought about life in the orphanage going on and on and on, with no end in sight. Or the fear they must have felt knowing that at sixteen they would "age out" of the orphanage with no hope and no future. They would have loved to know what they couldn't have known at that moment: that a family in a lovely land called Virginia was dreaming of them, making plans for them, anticipating them, and praying fervently for their arrival.

## The Story Behind All Stories

It was a great story, and it still is. Even more so because it's true.

As heartwarming as it may be, however, it is a reflection of a story even greater still. It's a story about me and a heavenly Father who loved me from afar and sought me across the galaxies, sacrificing to the utter limit of comprehension to obtain me for His own and bring me into His very household and family. Now *that's* a story.

In fact, it's a story so amazing that we have trouble grappling with such mind-numbing truth. God, of course, knows that. And that's one reason He loves to tell stories. Have you noticed? God highly favors the use of (sometimes startling) word pictures to make His point.

In the Old Testament books of prophecy, the God of Israel used picture after stunning picture, story after story to somehow reach the wandering, rebellious hearts of His people. Sometimes His metaphors were shocking and graphic, at other times tender and poignant. He wanted His people to understand the depths of His love for them, and He wanted to warn them of the dangers and sorrows that awaited them if they continued to walk in rebellion.

Jesus, of course, never stopped telling stories and sketching memorable word pictures. It was His favorite way of teaching. *"The kingdom of heaven is like a king who wanted to settle accounts with his servants.... The kingdom of heaven is like a landowner who went out early in the morning.... Suppose a woman has ten silver coins and loses one...."*

That's one of the reasons, I believe, why He leads us into God adventures along life's path. Through these real-life experiences, He paints a picture of His indescribable love. He teaches us more and more about His character and His plans for our lives. Those who stay in their safe routines and never risk climbing out of the rut don't seem to hear His voice as clearly as those who venture forth, leaning on His promises (and not much else).

As Andy and I walked through the process of adopting our girls, we found ourselves stunned by the parallels with God's work in our own lives. After all, the metaphor of adoption is one God particularly seems to like and uses again and again in the New Testament.

Please walk with me (for just a few moments) down our trail of discovery. Let me show you how responding to our Lord's call into adventure and faith can reveal His love and tenderness to us as never before.

## Adoption Insight #1:
## He Is Thinking About Me

The truth is, Andy and I were thinking about Alysa, Zoya, and Sophia before they ever thought of us—or even knew we existed. It touches me to remember that God thinks of you and me in the same way. In an incomprehensible realm beyond time and separated from the cares and sorrows of this world, there is a Father who thinks about us and a Savior who continually prays for us and longs for the day of our arrival on the Other Side.

We may only be dimly aware of this—if we think about it at all—but God is thinking about us as we live out our day-by-day world. As the *Message* paraphrase renders Jeremiah 29:11: "I know what I'm doing. I have it all planned out—plans to take care of you, not abandon you, plans to give you the future you hope for."

He's thinking about me. Planning for me. Charting out future God adventures for me. It's astonishing, but true. In Psalm 139, David declares, "How precious are your thoughts about me, O God! They are innumerable! I can't even count them; they outnumber the grains of sand!" (vv. 17–18, NLT).

And don't you love the story of Nathanael, daydreaming in the hot afternoon under a fig tree? Did he have any concept—any idea at all—that he was being carefully watched and considered in those moments? Jesus would say to him, "I saw you while you were still under the fig tree before Philip called you" (John 1:48).

In the same way, God was thinking of me long before I ever thought of Him. And even today, in times of confusion, pressure, or disappointment, He is thinking of me when I lose the handle on His presence, His love, and His watchful care over me.

He thought of me, and then He came looking for me. He had something wonderful planned—beyond my comprehension. If I had only known, I would have run to Him sooner.

## Adoption Insight #2:
## He Paid the Price

As I've mentioned, there was a time when our adoption paperwork got misplaced, and it looked as though our investment of thousands of dollars—as well as our time and our emotional energy—was going to be lost. We thought we would have to start the whole process over again from square one and that we would all have to wait who knows how long to be together as a family. But we would have pressed ahead anyway. We were willing to do whatever it took to get those three little lambs out of that orphanage and bring them under our roof and into our family.

There is really no way to compare the price we paid for the girls to the price Christ paid for us: "It was not with perishable things such as silver and gold that you were redeemed from the empty way of life handed down to you from your forefathers, but with the precious blood of Christ" (1 Peter 1:18–19).

We would say, "What price tag can you put on the value of a child's life?" And God looks at us and says, "There is no price too great to pay for you, My child."

Gordon Robertson, the executive producer and cohost of the *700 Club,* tells about a word Jesus spoke to his heart while he was in India. So very clearly, he heard the words, "Gordon, if you had been the only person, if you had been the only one in all the earth, I still would have come."

The price Jesus paid for us cannot be calculated— not in a trillion years. In fact, that one act of love became the very definition of the word: *"This is how we know what love is: Jesus Christ laid down his life for us"* (1 John 3:16).

## Adoption Insight #3:
## He Accepts Us, Then Cleans Us

We got in the car and drove away from the orphanage, my arms wrapped around three precious, excited girls.

But my new little daughters didn't smell like they belonged to me. They still smelled like the orphanage. They smelled "institutional," like the place they came from. But that wouldn't last for long—in fact, only until we got back to our hotel. We had brought all of those wonderful "girl things" they needed to make a new beginning. New clothes, new perfumed soap, new shampoo and conditioner, new lotion, new deodorant, new hairbrushes, toothpaste, and toothbrushes. And soon their hair began to shine. They began to smell fresh and sweet and to look radiant.

It came to me sometime later that we were like that, too, when we came to God. We smelled like the world, the place from which we'd come. He received us anyway—with all of our baggage and all the engrained soil and stains on our soul. The only way we could be cleaned up was to be washed in the blood of the Lord Jesus, so that we might stand before our Father, smelling clean and looking radiant. Peter tells us that Jesus brought us to God by dying for us: "For Christ also died for sins once for all, the just for the unjust, so that He might bring us to God" (1 Peter 3:18, NASB).

He cleans us, He fills us, He equips us, He robes us in white, and one day soon He will bring us into His home. We will be absolutely fit to live in heaven and stand in the presence of God—the very fountainhead of light and purity—and all His holy angels…because He Himself has made us ready.


ADOPTION INSIGHT #4:
HE GIVES ME A NEW NAME

When our girls' adoption became official, they kept their lovely Ukrainian first names; they're still Alysa, Zoya, and Sophia. Their last name, however, became our last name. They're ours now. They're one with us. They're part of our family. And they have new middle names, too. We gave them names that identified with our family; they're all named after significant women in our family.

God's Word tells us that He gives us a new name. Listen….

> You will be a crown of splendor in the LORD's hand,
> a royal diadem in the hand of your God.

No longer will they call you Deserted,
>   or name your land Desolate.
But you will be called Hephzibah ["My delight is in her"],
>   and your land Beulah ["married"];
for the LORD will take delight in you,
>   and your land will be married.

ISAIAH 62:3–4

Married to whom? Married to God. That means you now belong to Him. You bear His name, He is your protector and shield, and He delights to be near you and to shelter you.

I think about our girls, who had no hope, no future. They had suffered such loss and sadness and pain in their lives. Then, out of the blue, without them even suspecting anything was going to happen, we arrived at that orphanage. We arrived with a plan for them. We arrived with a purpose for their lives. We arrived with wide-open arms and invited them to join our family. And we gave them a new name—a name that came with a promise of protection and provision, a name that assured them of a hope and a future.

So it is with us. And how well I remember. Before Jesus came into my life, I too might have been called "Deserted" and "Desolate." I was so broken and felt so alone. But Jesus Christ arrived on the scene (out of the blue). He invited me to be His, He embraced me, and He cleaned me up. Because of His great care for me and by His grace, I am looking more and more like I really belong to His family. He has committed Himself to me and delights in me. He has given me His name, which means a hope and a future and an inheritance more glorious than I can begin to conceive.

Remember the words of the apostle John?

> What marvelous love the Father has extended to us! Just look at it—we're called children of God! That's who we really are.... And that's only the beginning. Who knows how we'll end up! What we know is that when Christ is openly revealed, we'll see him—and in seeing him, become like him.
>
> I  J O H N  3 : 1 – 2 ,  *T H E  M E S S A G E*

God's inheritance to us is all of who He is, and all of what He has. It is His passionate love reaching out to us from before the beginning of time. Before we ever knew He was there, He was loving us and preparing a place for us.

Time has passed in our family, and our girls have thrived in an atmosphere of love, acceptance, and security. There will still be issues from their past that they will continue to confront and deal with through the years, but the darkness and pain of those bygone days will fade and shrink in prominence with every passing year.

They are loved. They are protected. They are provided for and prayed for. They are family.

Andy and I are so very, very grateful we stepped far, far beyond our comfort zone a few years ago and followed God into an adventure that changed our lives and certainly the lives of our children—all seven of them—forever. We have a strong sense that this adventure is still unfolding. That it is bigger than we can even understand or imagine right now. We are thankful to be part of it.

The more we think about what took place in that process of adoption, the more we are awed to consider what took place in *our* adoption, when heaven stepped into our dark world, right out of the blue.

That's the way it is with a God adventure.

So how about you? What is God speaking to your heart today? Perhaps the biggest question is...*are you listening?* Recently when I was in South Africa, I was told of an older man who had finally become a believer. His family had prayed for him for years. Shortly after committing his life to Christ he was diagnosed with a terminal illness and given just two months to live. He had the peace and certainty of knowing where he would spend eternity, and his family was so relieved and thankful for that. But the last weeks of his life were filled with remorse over the knowledge that he had missed all of God's plans for his life on this side of heaven. What a tragedy!

It doesn't have to be that way. His arms are open to you…right now.

Wedding day... When Andy and I married, we committed ourselves to be risk-takers for the Lord.

When Tyler arrived, we celebrated the gift of a new son—and J. P. was our own "wise man from the east."

We loved our heaven-assembled family...and assumed God had completed the work He had begun. Little did we know that, years later, He would be adding to the mix yet again—in a big way!

God has created each of His children with a different bent, diverse interests, and unique passions and joys. This becomes evident early on with the choice of playthings!

"Survivors"! Every family needs to find its way through the jungle of learning, discipline, and loving each other through the fun times *and* hard times. We had no idea of the challenge that soon awaited us!

Zoya, Sophia, and Alysa, standing in the office of the orphanage director. This was the first picture of "our girls" we were able to obtain. Our hearts ached to take them out of that place that very moment—but we had to wait five long months before we met them for the first time.

In summer camp, months before we arrived to claim them, the girls had no idea of the major life changes that awaited them just down the road.

Once upon a time...three innocent little Ukrainian girls were taken from their home and placed in an orphanage. It was a sad chapter of their lives, but God had wonderful chapters ahead for them—and for us.

"A new papa" with an armload of happy girls. We couldn't help but think of how our loving heavenly Father adopted us—orphaned and alone as we were—into His very family circle.

Together at last! Our God adventure took us halfway around the world and changed our family forever…and it has really only begun.

Less than a month after arriving back home in November 2002, we posed for our annual Christmas card photo. Only this year, our family was suddenly half again bigger than the year before.

Tory found herself with three new sisters…and the girls in our family suddenly outnumbered the boys. Photo courtesy of Eva Freyss (www.fotobyeva.com)

Alysa…one year after joining our family.
Photo courtesy of Eva Freyss (www.fotobyeva.com)

Zoya…one year after
joining our family.
Photo courtesy of Eva Freyss
(www.fotobyeva.com)

Sophia…one year after joining our family. Photo
courtesy of Eva Freyss (www.fotobyeva.com)

The whole gang…each a unique and wonderful gift from the Lord. Photo courtesy of Eva Freyss (www.fotobyeva.com)

What a ride it has been! What an incredible God adventure. I wouldn't have missed it for the world.

# Learn from the Past... and Let It Go

I run in the path of your commands,

for you have set my heart free.

PSALM 119:32

7

WHAT IF TODAY, right out of the clear blue sky, or tonight, out under the stars, God placed before you a clear-cut opportunity for an adventure in faith with Him?

Are you ready? Ready to lace up your shoes, step through that door, and follow Him?

Why do we shy away from open doors, from the prospect of new adventures in faith? Why do we let opportunity after opportunity pass us by, even though we feel a stirring of desire and a tug on our hearts to respond? What holds us back?

I think many of us are simply too weighed down and tangled up by our past to step into God's purpose today. How sad. We lose "today" because of "yesterday." Life flows on by and age creeps up on us while we remain mired in doubts, fears, and hesitations.

Have you ever met some older person, now physically unable to work or travel, who could only look back on life with regrets? It's not a happy story. Some older man will say, "Years ago, I had the opportunity to serve the Lord overseas—and deep down, I really wanted to go. But I had a good job, and I was climbing the ladder. So I held back. Then the opportunity passed me by—and it never came again." Or some older lady saying, "My husband and I couldn't have children. He wanted to adopt a baby girl from China, but I was afraid. I kept stalling the decision, and we never did. Now my husband's gone, and here I am with no one in my life. It would be so wonderful to have a daughter."

Life is too short to live with regrets! Life is too precious to turn away from promising opportunities to serve the King in His kingdom. The psalmist said, "I run in the path of your commands, for you have set my heart free" (Psalm 119:32). That's what we want. To just run and run and run into His will and the paths of His purpose. With a light heart, a clear eye, and hope rushing bank-high through the channels of our heart. But we can't run if we have huge packs on our backs or ropes tangling up our feet. Let's consider a few of the reasons why we allow our past to hold us back and keep us from embracing God adventures.

## Obstacle #1:
## Our Past Sins and Failures

Our sins and our offenses against God and others are so fresh in our minds that we groan to remember them. We remember the many times we have failed, made poor choices, or stumbled off the path into the brush and the briars. We count up our own sins against ourselves. The enemy, too, keeps tabs on all our hypocrisies and transgressions.

The only One who doesn't seem to be marking those sins against us is the very One who has the greatest right to do so. The psalmist wrote:

> If You, LORD, should mark iniquities,
> > O Lord, who could stand?
> But there is forgiveness with You,
> > That You may be feared.
>
> PSALM 130:3−4, NASB

What could be more wondrous than this? We have a God who inhabits eternity, who looks down upon time and sees our future as clearly as He sees our past. There is no detail in the universe—past, present, or future—that escapes His notice and scrutiny. There are no secret sins. In fact, "everything is uncovered and laid bare before the eyes of him to whom we must give account" (Hebrews 4:13). Yet the Bible tells us that when we ask and receive forgiveness from this all-seeing God, He removes our sin "as far as the east is from the west" and He will "remember [our] sins no more" (Psalm 103:12; Jeremiah 31:34).

How could that be? Does God have selective memory? Apparently when it comes to our sins—covered by the blood of His Son—He does. He chooses not to remember those things we've confessed to Him, or ever bring them to mind. He chooses not to identify us by our stumbling blocks—those flaws, embarrassments, and betrayals the world would gladly attach to our name and the enemy so delights to remind us of at every opportunity. Our lives may be like an open book before Him, but when it comes to confessed sin, those pages become invisible.

"If You, LORD, should mark iniquities...."

But He doesn't! We might, but He doesn't. Others try, but He refrains. Satan will, but He won't. He isn't counting up our sins against us. He doesn't keep a scorecard of our failures and broken promises. He isn't saving up our secret transgressions to spring on us someday in court. In fact, He is for us. And "if God is for us, who can be against us? Who will bring any charge against those whom God has chosen? It is God who justifies. Who is he that condemns? Christ Jesus, who died—more than that, who was raised to life—is at the right hand of God and is also interceding for us" (Romans 8:31, 33–34).

In other words, He not only chooses not to remember our crimes; He also provides the counsel for our defense when the accuser throws his charges at us.

Even so, it is often a journey to come to that point of accepting myself in Christ the same way God accepts me in Christ. The wrong choices we have made—and the wrong choices of others that have damaged us—are like weights upon our ankles and lead encasing our soul. Rather than running, we find ourselves *dragging* our way along those pathways of God's purpose.

Jesus, however, says that when you know the truth, the truth will set you free. What truth? Just this: When you allow the Lord Jesus to live His life through you by the power of the indwelling Holy Spirit, you can honestly say, "I am ready for anything and equal to anything through Him Who infuses inner strength into me; I am self-sufficient in Christ's sufficiency" (Philippians 4:13, AMP).

Don't let the scars of your past become your identity. When you receive Christ as Lord and Savior, you become a brand-new creation. In other words, nothing in my past can keep me from meeting any life challenge when I allow Jesus to infuse (I love that word!) His strength into my inmost being.

## Obstacle #2:
## Our Old Dreams and Expectations

"To everything there is a season," wrote Solomon, "a time for every purpose under heaven." He went on to explain that there is "a time to keep, and a time to throw away" (Ecclesiastes 3:1, 6, NKJV).

For some of us, it's time to do some very personal housecleaning and get rid of some old dreams. It's time to put away some long-held and treasured expectations...*and move on with life.* In the book of Isaiah, the Lord told His people:

> "Forget the former things;
> > do not dwell on the past.
> See, I am doing a new thing!
> > Now it springs up; do you not perceive it?
> I am making a way in the desert
> > and streams in the wasteland."

> 43:18–19

He says the same thing to you and me. But how can we possibly see what new things God desires to accomplish in our lives if we are always focused on "the former things" and "dwell on the past"? We feel discouraged and blue, as if we were living in a barren wilderness. But if we would only open our eyes, we would see that He is making a way through that desert and causing fresh streams to flow through the wasteland!

I love this passage. The Lord is saying, "Wake up. Don't keep looking back. Don't go on dreaming about the past, the way things were, or the way you expected or hoped they would be. Don't you think I'm a God who can create something new? Don't you think I can bring fresh experiences, new friends, and worthwhile challenges into your life? You think life has become one big gray desert, and you're depressed and sad. But look up! Lift up your eyes! I can create a way where you thought there was no way. I can cause springs of joy to bubble up right out of the dry, rocky ground."

Many of our old dreams, if we honestly examined them, have a lot of self-promotion involved in them. But God has something better for us—something that may be very, very different from what we would choose for ourselves. But He won't replace those old

*The God Adventure*

dreams until we're willing to let them go. He won't enter into a power struggle or tug-of-war with us, pulling back and forth between our plan and His plan, our way and His way. He will simply wait...until you and I are ready to pry our fingers off of those old hopes, dreams, and expectations and cast ourselves completely upon Him and His plan for our lives.

Letting go... I've certainly had the desire to do that at different moments in the past. I will place some treasured expectation onto the altar of sacrifice—only to grip it all over again before I've even finished the prayer. Still worrying about it, manipulating it, controlling it, and trying to direct it where I want it to go.

Is God angry with me about that? No, He knows it's a process with us. He understands our flesh. "He knows how we are formed, he remembers that we are dust" (Psalm 103:14). Even so, if you want to experience His joy and the refreshment of new adventures in faith, keep handing those old things over until you are free from them. Keep praying for release. Keep asking the Holy Spirit for the power and strength and grace and courage to let go. The Bible recognizes the "process" of our faith walk when it says we "work out [our] salvation with fear and trembling" (Philippians 2:12). Not a word about it being easy.

## Obstacle #3:
## Our Unwillingness to Forgive

Perhaps the key to letting loose of some of the things that need to be released in your life is your willingness to forgive. I can think of at least two very critical times in my life when a willingness to forgive had everything to do with my finding freedom in Christ and moving on.

The first was the rape incident I mentioned in chapter 2—and the subsequent struggle to forgive—which brought me to my knees and to faith in Jesus Christ. That shameful act of violence brought with it all the emotions you might imagine: a sense of violation, an attack on my privacy, my rights, my very personhood. Everything about that incident cried out for anger, and for retaliation.

I had to make a choice about that. Was I going to put my focus on this man, who out of his own woundedness had violated me? What could I do? Where could I go with the humiliation, pain, and shame?

I wasn't a believer in those days. I was a very self-sufficient, hard-nosed young woman consumed with chasing my own dreams and my own self-promotion. The way I saw it, I really didn't need God; I was managing things quite well by myself.

But then *this*...an incident that shattered me emotionally and physically. And in those days of brokenness, I found myself willing to listen to someone speak about something beyond my experience. God sent people into my life to share the message of His love at just the right time—when my heart was tender and my need was great. I heard the gospel message and I yearned to respond.

But how could I accept the forgiveness of God if I refused to forgive the man who had violated me? It had nothing to do with whether he was asking for my forgiveness, or whether he was even sorry for what he'd done to me. It had everything to do with my willingness to obey God.

So in the process of offering forgiveness, I found forgiveness...and the freedom I'd been looking for my whole life. But I never could have moved on into the life God had for me—I never could have tasted the countless adventures of walking with Him—until I left that bitterness and anger behind me.

God's timing is always perfect. Do I think He orchestrated that rape? Of course not. Do I think He allowed it to happen in my life and used it to bring me to Himself? Yes, I do. And on this side of it, so many years later (and as strange as it sounds), I can honestly say that I'm grateful.

The second incident centered around my divorce—something I had never, never wanted. Between dating and marriage, I had shared eight years of my life with this man. I had to choose what I was going to do with my thoughts and emotions toward someone I deeply loved, but who in many ways had violated me more personally than the rapist. Without going into detail here, it was a betrayal of trust, a betrayal of my love, a betrayal of every vow we'd made to each other. What was I going to do with that? How was I going to let go?

God knows how I hated the whole thought of divorce. I dreaded it. Feared it like some great dragon lurking in the darkness before me. From my first waking impressions until my head hit the pillow at night, I could think of nothing else. The experience colored my hours and shaped my days.

Then the dragon pounced, and I found myself right in the middle of where I never wanted to be: a divorce from the man I loved. Did God really expect me to just forgive my husband for crushing my heart and shredding my life?

Yes, He did.

Would I do it? Could I do it? Could I walk in obedience to His Word when all of my emotions wanted to walk—to run—the other way?

Yes, in His strength, I could.

When I offered forgiveness in my heart to the man who was about to become my ex-husband, it certainly wasn't because I *felt* like doing it. It wasn't because it seemed right or just or the logical thing to do. It was only because I needed to follow my Lord in obedience.

And when I did, when I set my face to obey Him, walking against the gale force of my emotions, an amazing thing happened. Healing began to warm my life like soft morning sunlight. And God began opening paths of opportunity beyond what I could have ever imagined.

If you have faced or are facing such terrible, tearing circumstances in your life, I want to affirm that God will honor the sacrifice of your obedience. Your thoughts and emotions will follow, after you've been obedient— but probably not before. As you keep relinquishing to God your "rights" to these feelings of unforgivingness, as you keep laying it on the altar before Him, He will acknowledge and honor that sacrifice.

In both cases, after forgiving the man who raped me and the man who betrayed and divorced me, I found a freedom to move on into the things God was calling me to. With the psalmist, I began to run in the path of His commands because He had set my heart free.

When it's all said and done, our brief life on this planet, under this sun, is a training ground, preparing us for an eternity of serving the King. Life is all about the choices we make here on earth. Your life circumstances may look very, very different from mine, but in the end it all boils down to those all-important decisions we make—often in the times of great pressure or distress. Will we allow our feelings and our desires to rule us, or will we allow the living Christ to rule us? When we finally come to know Him as Lord of our lives, and not just the Savior of our souls, we begin to shape our choices out of obedience and love. He is the One who sacrificed everything for us. He brought us back from a far country, He lifted us out of the pit, and He established us as His own children in the kingdom of light. Obeying Him in these difficult areas is our way of saying thank You, our way of acknowledging the price He paid to buy our lives out of slavery and despair.

The enemy will always try to convince you that what has happened to you in the past defines your future. But that is a lie—straight from the father of lies. It is the grace and power of God that defines your future, and your willingness to embrace His good plan for your life. *Your past is not your future.* As a child of the King of kings and Lord of lords, you have a future that's beyond imagining, and it's available to you for the asking. Don't miss it!

## RELEASED BY THE SPIRIT'S POWER

What we've been talking about in this chapter is something infinitely more powerful than mental discipline or some extraordinary resolution of the human will. In my own strength, I could have never escaped my anger and bitterness toward those two men who wounded me. The hurts were too deep; the memories were too scarred. I needed a power beyond my own to break away from the strong backward suction of past devastations.

I needed the supernatural enabling of the Holy Spirit.

He is the One, living in the very center of our being, who gives us the ability to step with boldness and freedom into each new tomorrow. Think of Peter, in the book of Acts. How could he ever escape from the knowledge that in his Lord's great hour of peril, he had totally caved in to fear and denied that he even knew Jesus? That's the kind of craven betrayal that could very well have defined and limited Peter's life for all his days.

Yet just a few weeks later, Peter stands eyeball to eyeball before a huge and hostile multitude—including those who had just crucified Jesus—and fearlessly declares salvation in Christ. *What happened?* What turned a fearful, discouraged, humiliated former fisherman into a roaring tiger for Jesus Christ?

Pentecost. That's what happened.

The Holy Spirit fell upon the waiting disciples— Peter, too—and literally ignited them, flames dancing over their heads. They were *transformed* from fear-filled, quaking followers of Jesus hiding behind closed doors into bold, eloquent evangelists. They moved from their dark, confining room right out onto the balcony to declare the truth they had found to anyone who would listen! They didn't take tentative, mincing steps into a new God adventure; they sprinted into their new life. That's what the Holy Spirit can do!

Paul, too, the former Saul of Tarsus: a hunter and murderer of Christians…that is, until he had a radical encounter with Jesus. An encounter that stopped him in his tracks and threw him to the ground. An encounter that challenged everything he believed and knew. The Lord sent Ananias to lay hands on Paul, and his eyes were opened and he was filled with the Holy Spirit. Radically transformed, Paul did an about-face and began proclaiming the deity of Christ, joining the very believers he had come to destroy. But God didn't just reveal to Paul the wrongness of his ways. He didn't just open his eyes to the truth of who Jesus is. Ananias prayed that Paul would be filled with the Holy Spirit. Webster says the verb *fill* means "to occupy the whole of...to spread through; to make full." God supernaturally changed and empowered Paul by His Holy Spirit.

How would you like to have the imprisonment and deaths of scores—perhaps hundreds—of innocent Christian men and women on your conscience? Paul could have lived out his life as a tortured soul after he saw the light on the Damascus road. He could have kept a low profile, shunned the public eye, and walked a lonely road with his regrets. Instead, he proclaimed the faith from town to town, marketplace to marketplace, out to the very edges of the known world. He stepped into the lives of dozens of believers and mentored young pastors with great tenderness and love.

Where did he find such confidence? How was he able to leave his past behind and stride boldly into new God adventures all over the world?

It was the Holy Spirit, alive within him. Filling him with the very power of God. He is the one who keeps us focused on the work and opportunities before us *today*.

Can't you just see that battered and beaten apostle

smiling as he wrote these words? "May the God of hope FILL you with all joy and peace as you trust in him, so that you may overflow with hope *by the power of the Holy Spirit*" (Romans 15:13).

God's Spirit can take any of us, no matter what our past, no matter what our track record, no matter what tragedies have crashed into our lives, and cause us to absolutely brim over with power, with joy and peace, trust and hope.

You may not think so right now. Your emotions may shout a very different message. Just take that first baby step of obedience, no matter how your emotions rebel…and ask God's mighty Spirit to transform you and empower you. You may be overwhelmed with the impossibility of it all.

I remember. That's how I felt, too.

*The God Adventure*

# Find the Treasure

# in Today

*"Today, if you hear his voice,*
*do not harden your hearts."*

HEBREWS 4:7

8

FACEDOWN BEFORE a mysterious ball of fire in the desert, Moses was unprepared for the reality of that moment. He simply could not believe what his senses were telling him. God was speaking to him. *God!* From a bush. Through flames that burned but did not consume. When had such a thing ever happened? And as if that weren't enough, God was in the middle of giving him an impossible commission.

What was He saying? Go one-on-one with the most powerful ruler in the world? Lead a whole nation out of slavery? Impossible! Almost laughable. Except Moses wasn't laughing; he was lying prone in the sand, trying to comprehend how such an ordinary day had turned into a day like no other. And even as God gave him specific directions for the trip to Egypt, Moses' mind cycled back to the past: his terrible failures, his poor decisions, his wasted potential, his broken dreams.

Maybe that's why God chose that moment to share

*The God Adventure*

His name with the old shepherd. He said, "I am who I am. This is what you are to say to the Israelites: 'I AM has sent me.'" God didn't say, "I was," or "I will be." He said, *"I Am."* He is the God of today. He is eternally present. All that He is, He is right now. He brings His might and wisdom and glory and compassion to this very moment in time…where *we* live.

Today.

Like Moses, we often focus on the past. Where we've been. What we've experienced. What we know for sure. What we have achieved or how we have miserably failed. But God, I AM WHO I AM, wants us to trust Him *today,* to rely on His power and grace and guidance *today,* and follow where He leads, no matter what your previous track record…and even if His commission seems impossible.

## GRACE FOR THE MOMENT

Today is a wondrous day.

I love that little saying you see now and then on a refrigerator magnet or someone's T-shirt. *Today is a gift. That's why it's called the present.* If you are reading these words, God has given you life this day. Today is yours. In all of human history, this is your time, your moment. You have life. You have opportunities before you that have never existed before and may never exist again. And if you know Jesus as your Savior, you have the almighty God of the universe to be your guide. He has given you the living Holy Spirit who personally indwells your life. And "whether you turn to the right or to the left, your ears will hear a voice behind you, saying, 'This is the way; walk in it'" (Isaiah 30:21).

How could today ever be anything less than a miracle? *God* is here.

How could today ever be hopeless, no matter what the circumstances? God is here, and He is the God of hope.

As Paul wrote, "May the God of hope fill you with all joy and peace as you trust in him, so that you may overflow with hope by the power of the Holy Spirit" (Romans 15:13).

God inhabits the here and now. He is the eternal I Am. And He can do *anything*. You don't have to explain your situation or the extenuating circumstances to Him; from His point of view, it's not complicated at all—and He knows the details better than you do. You don't have to get out your scrapbook and remind Him about your past washouts or your big moments; He was with you in your past and is acquainted with all your ways. You don't have to stress about tomorrow or the day after that, because *He is already there.* He has gone ahead of you and will prepare the way for you.

It's difficult for us as limited, finite creatures to comprehend a God who is above time, who is unrestricted and unhindered by time. He's already in your tomorrow. Think of it! He's looking at your future this very moment. He has walked where you will one day walk, experienced what you will one day experience, and pondered situations in your life that have yet to be. He's not going to drop you. He's not going to forget you. He's not going to lose your file. He's not going to let go of your hand when you find yourself in trouble or sorrow—even of your own making. Instead, He is going to lift you and carry you through whatever this day—and all your days—may hold.

So here you are, neck deep in the middle of "today," facing...whatever. And either God is God, and He is sufficient for *this* precise moment, for *this* precise set of circumstances, or He isn't God at all. The Bible says, "God is able to make all grace abound to you, so that *in all things at all times,* having all that you need, you will abound in every good work" (2 Corinthians 9:8).

Perhaps you woke up this morning feeling overwhelmed by your situation. Everything seems new and strange. You feel like the odds against you are impossible.

This is exactly where the God adventure begins, because He specializes in the impossible. He doesn't start with the things we're *able* to do for Him. He starts with the impossible—or at least the wildly improbable—and asks us to join Him in an adventure of faith.

God is looking for a willingness in our hearts, just as He was with Moses at the burning bush. He's looking for a readiness to walk with Him, to do it His way, to go in the direction He's going. Instead of coming to Him and asking Him to rubber-stamp our plans for the day, He wants us to ask, "What do You have in mind, Father? What does today's adventure look like? What is it You want to do with me today, with my life, with my circumstances? How do You want me to use the blessings You've given me? Who do You want me to reach out to today? What could You do in me and through me if I gave You all of me?"

Very few people want to let go of their agenda to grab hold of God's. It's hard to grab hold of anything if your hands are already full.

## Excess Baggage

Nancy, a friend of mine, experienced a serious illness that kept her confined for weeks to her bed or easy chair. An active lady and a meticulous housekeeper, she grieved not being able to move around the house and do all those tasks that really needed doing.

One day a group of friends arrived on her doorstep. But they didn't bring cards and flowers and casseroles. They brought brooms, dust mops, buckets, and scrub brushes. They told Nancy, "We want to come and bless you today." And without a further word, they set to work cleaning her house.

I'm sure you'll understand my friend's mixed emotions. On the one hand, she was humbled and grateful to have such friends, so willing to roll up their sleeves and sacrifice their time. On the other hand, it pained her to watch them. This was *her* house. She wanted to be the one cleaning, polishing, scrubbing, and re-arranging. It was hard to sit in a chair and watch others take over her responsibilities.

It was particularly galling when one of the women placed herself in charge of a closet in the front hall. All of us probably have at least one closet like that one. (In fact, I just cleaned one out a few weeks ago.) It was stuffed to the brim with items that she wasn't using "but might be useful someday"—and seemed too valuable to just give away.

This particular friend—with the best of intentions—took it upon herself to clean out that closet and free up the space for Nancy. And the more she cleaned, unearthing item after item, the more uncomfortable Nancy became. *I don't like her looking through my things,* Nancy thought. *But what can I say? These ladies are being so good to me.*

As the woman began pulling out objects and heaping them in an untidy pile, Nancy's discomfort turned into irritation. "I'm going to pile these things on the floor here," the woman said, "and I want you to send these to Goodwill. You don't need these things anymore, Nancy. They haven't seen the light of day for years, right? We're going to give you a whole new space and help you get organized."

The more this friend talked, the more indignant Nancy became. *What right does she have coming into my house and hauling my things out of my own closet? Who is she to decide what I will use and what I won't use? I'm not going to say anything, but as soon as she leaves it's all going back right where it came from!*

She consoled herself with these thoughts as the friends wrapped up their cleaning ministry. Finally, they gathered their supplies, each gave Nancy a hug, and left her alone in the house again. Summoning her strength, Nancy hobbled over to the closet and looked down at that eclectic mound of possessions on the floor of an otherwise sparkling house. She began sort-

*The God Adventure*

ing through them, with the idea of cramming them all back on the shelves.

In that moment, the Lord spoke to her.

He seemed to say in her heart, "Nancy, don't put *any* of those things back into that closet. I want you to give them away."

*But Lord,* she argued, *they're usable. There's nothing wrong with them. Why should I just give them away? They're perfectly good things.*

"Yes," the Lord said to her, "they're perfectly good. But they are not what I have purposed for you anymore. I want to do a new thing in your life. I am cleaning out those things from your closet, just as I am cleaning some things from your heart and life through this season of illness and trial. I am removing them because I have something better that I want to give you. And as long as you keep holding on to the clutter from the past, you won't have room for My gifts. *Let go, Nancy.* Let Me remove from your heart, from your mind, from your life, those things that I'm trying to strip away so that I can give you what is best."

We have trouble with this thought, don't we? We want to cling to yesterday's blessings, yesterday's plans, yesterday's dreams, yesterday's methods, yesterday's successes, yesterday's way of looking at things. We want to search our cupboards for crumbs of yesterday's manna, rather than stepping outside to see how God might provide for us today.

Sometimes we hang on so tightly to what has been that we have no room in our lives for what God wants to do *today*, this wondrous day that lies before us. Sometimes God wants to rid you of the good in order to give you the best. Don't fight Him on that. He has a purpose and a plan, and His plan is good.

My friend came to realize that she had excess baggage in her life—baggage that was weighing her down and keeping her from fresh adventures of faith.

As Nancy discovered, excess baggage can consist of good, worthy, useful things. But if we find that those preconceptions, commitments, and comfortable life patterns are keeping us from what God wants to bring into our lives today, then the extra luggage has to go. That which was once useful and good has become a snare and a stumbling block to us.

Maybe it's a Bible study you've taught for years. You've done it for so long that it feels natural and comfortable—like an old slipper. Are you willing to let go of it and try something new if you sense God's Spirit nudging you on?

Perhaps God wants you to move to a new area—or even a different country—but you've been unwilling to consider it. You have family and friends nearby, you're in a great church, or you're living in a wonderful part of the country. It's where your roots are. It's familiar. It's home. Are you willing, like Abraham, to leave everything and follow God into a land you've never seen?

Maybe He is calling you to come close to someone at work, or one of your relatives, shunned by the rest of the family. Yet stepping across that line to seek this individual out may mean letting go of your comfort zone, letting go of your privacy. It may mean surrendering your desire to stay in a safe place, at a safe distance. Are you willing to let go of life as it was yesterday, to embrace God's plan for today?

God may be seeking to release us, to pry our clutching fingers from some of those good things that we have passionately embraced in our lives, in order to use us in new and mighty ways. He may want to pour new wine from our lives, though we keep telling ourselves "the old is better."

Today is a gift, and we should enjoy everything that God has given us. But we should also live this day with an open hand, knowing that at any time He may radically change our circumstances. He may ask us to move into a new place and do a new work for Him, with enabling beyond what we have ever experienced before. When we agree to walk into unknown territory with Him, we discover aspects of God's character and power and love that we never knew existed. Every adventure is an opportunity to know Him more.

You may have never been someone who has expected God to move in you, around you, and through you to touch the lives of others.

Today is the day to change those expectations.

Today is the day when the eternal *I AM*, the mighty God, the Lord of the now, will move you into a fresh adventure of faith…if you are willing to follow Him step-by-step.

It really begins by simply asking Him to make the most of today in your life. It begins by giving Him total freedom to send you through any door He wants to open, no matter where it leads. It begins by asking Him to give you a vision for what He wants you to do in your sphere of influence, the circle of your being, the world you live in. And if He speaks to your heart and begins to nudge you in a new direction, ask Him to open your spiritual ears and the eyes of your understanding so that you can begin to grasp what He's telling you. And then hold onto that vision tenaciously.

Most likely, the enemy will come in like a flood. He wants you to stay where you are. He wants to keep you in a rut. He's not going to let you embark on a God adventure without a battle. But if God has given you the vision, He will also guard you and sustain you as you lean on Him. The battle belongs to the Lord. I love the words to this praise song:

> The victory is mine,
>> when the battle is the Lord's.
> Hosanna! Hosanna!
> No enemy can stand when
>> His Word goes forth—
> Hosanna! Hosanna!

A God adventure begins when He sets a challenge before you that you know you cannot meet unless He shows up and does something radical. We are nothing without Him. He is the Vine that gives life to our branch; He is the Living Bread that gives strength for our journey.

Choose to follow Him. Choose eternity over time. Choose to walk in the excitement of the new pathways God has purposed for you rather than the comfort and certainty of what you can see right now. Only God can reveal the unimaginable possibilities of...today.

Don't miss it, for in all of time and eternity, it will never come again.

Don't miss the great adventure of His call on your life.

Hosanna! Hosanna!

# God's Leading

*By an act of faith, Abraham said yes to God's call*

*to travel to an unknown place that would become his home.*

*When he left he had no idea where he was going.*

HEBREWS 11:8, *THE MESSAGE*

9

HOW CAN WE KNOW if a God adventure is really a
God adventure? How can we be sure that what we
think we hear Him saying is actually His voice, His
plan, His desire for our lives?

That's a very important question. I, for one, would
never want to launch out into the blue without the
assurance that I am stepping into God's purpose and
have His covering and blessing. Being "well-intentioned"
or "sincere" isn't going to cut it when the pressure begins
to flatten you like a bug on the windshield. When the
inevitable storms sweep suddenly over the horizon, you
want to make sure you're on the path of God's choosing,
not your own.

It makes me think of what God told Jeremiah
one time. The prophet had been complaining to the
Lord about the kind of people he had to deal with
and how hard his job had been: *"Why do bad people
have it so good? Why do con artists make it big? How*

long do we have to put up with this?" The Lord lis-
tened to His servant for a while and then replied,
"So, Jeremiah, if you're worn out in this footrace
with men, what makes you think you can race
against horses? And if you can't keep your wits during times of calm, what's going to happen when
troubles break loose like the Jordan in flood?"
(Jeremiah 12:1, 4–5, *The Message*).

If Jeremiah was going to survive the hard times
ahead, he needed to go back and revisit his calling. He
needed to remember that day when the word of the
Lord came to him and the Spirit of God filled his heart
and commissioned him for service... *"Before I shaped
you in the womb, I knew all about you. Before you saw
the light of day, I had holy plans for you: A prophet to the
nations—that's what I had in mind for you"* (Jeremiah
1:5, *The Message*).

When the heat is really on, you need to be sure
that you are in His will, on His mission, and walking
in His wisdom and power. Then, as the old saying
goes, "Don't doubt in the darkness what God has
shown you in the light!"

I think there are a number of ways that we can test
the waters before we plunge headfirst into a God
adventure.

## "Multitude of Counselors"

When I felt like the Lord first spoke to me in my quiet time about the girls coming, I knew that I needed confirmation from someone. It seemed like such a crazy idea. Was I crazy?

First of all, I went to my dear friend Julie Jenney, who produces *Living the Life,* one of the programs I host on CBN. Since she already knew about the girls' story, I poured out my thoughts to her and what I thought the Lord might be asking my family to do. "Would you please pray about this?" I pleaded. "And would you just tell me if you think I'm crazy?"

Immediately her eyes welled up with tears. She looked at me, hugged me, and said, "No, Terry, I don't think you are crazy."

Next I went to Rhonda Palser, my personal assistant here at CBN. "Rhonda," I said, "you're going to think I've really lost it this time. But I want to tell you what I feel like God is saying to me." And I shared the word that I felt God had given to my heart.

Rhonda's eyes brimmed with tears. "No, Terry," she said. "I don't think you've lost it. I don't think you're crazy at all. And yes, of course I'll pray about this with you."

Finally, I talked to my husband, Andy, as I've

*The God Adventure*

already described. Then my children, who would be just as affected by the decision as Andy and me. Truthfully, I didn't know how they would respond. They might have easily said, "Are you kidding? No way! We don't want the hassles, we don't want the inconveniences, and we don't want to share our parents and our home with three kids we don't even know." But instead they said, "Go ahead, Mom and Dad. It's the right thing to do."

I really wondered what kind of response I would get when I talked to my sister. This is a lady who knows me inside and out—knows my life, knows my marriage, and knows how wild and chaotic it can get around our house with the four children we already have. We were walking around our neighborhood in the dark, and I asked her, "Do you think I've lost my mind?"

I couldn't see her face in the dark, but I remember there was a slight hesitation and then a quiver in her voice when she spoke.

"No, Terry. I don't think you've lost your mind. I'm just jealous."

God kept confirming our decision again and again. I gave Him so many chances to slam the door on this God adventure, but He kept declining to do it!

Back at the *700 Club*, I went to Gordon Robertson, a man I work with every day. I shared the story with him, too—beginning to end—and asked him to pray with me. He needed to understand that if I undertook this adventure, it would have an impact on my television work. "Gordon," I said, "will you come alongside me as far as letting me take time off to go to Ukraine?"

Again, God could have easily closed the door right there. Things can be pressured and hectic at the network with a full staff. What would it be like if one of the hosts stepped out of the picture for a while?

"Terry," Gordon said, "we want to come alongside you in any way we can. What you are doing—this is the heart of Jesus."

To be honest, I kept looking for someone who would say, "Terry Meeuwsen, what in the world are you thinking of? You're insane to even consider this! Go take a cold shower, drink a cup of strong coffee, and don't even think about this anymore!" *Somewhere, I thought, someone will wave a big red flag. Someone will say, "I have a check in my spirit about this." Because this is not a normal thing for a couple in their fifties to be thinking about.* But every person from beginning to end kept saying go, go, go.

It won't always be that way, of course. Not everyone will applaud the vision or adventure God has placed in your heart. What do you imagine Abraham's relatives back in Ur must have said to him when he put his house on the market, packed up everything he had, and headed off into the complete unknown? *"Abe, Abe. Have you ever thought of getting a prescription for Prozac?"* There will be those who are not walking with the Lord, or who aren't in tune with His Spirit, and they will see your situation from a worldly, human-logic point of view. There will be people who tell you that you are crazy for following Christ.

But what you need to look for is a *pattern of responses* among those whom you truly respect, among those you know to be mature in the Lord and in the Word of God. If you go from godly person to godly person and get virtually the same answer, if you see a pattern of green lights as you seek counsel, then keep moving forward. All the while, however, keep praying, *Lord, I just want what You want. If You don't want me to go this direction, I will be obedient. Please close the door, remove the desire, make this impossible, or redirect me into the path of Your choosing.*

The Bible says we are to do this, to seek wise counsel.

Where there is no counsel, the people fall;
But in the multitude of counselors there is safety.

PROVERBS 11:14, NKJV

*God's Leading*

143

Without counsel plans fail,
but with many advisers they succeed.

PROVERBS 15:22, ESV

For by wise counsel you will wage your own
war, And in a multitude of counselors there is
safety.

PROVERBS 24:6, NKJV

One more thing...don't be afraid of what these
counselors might tell you. If it's stretching, be
stretched. If it's cautious, slow down. If it's urgent, then
don't delay. Let God speak to you through His wise
and mature sons and daughters. That's part of the
value of being a member of God's family.

## "A LAMP TO MY FEET...A LIGHT FOR MY PATH"

As you search the Scriptures daily, ask the Holy Spirit
to reveal the mind of the Lord to you. Ask Him to
speak to you through the written Word and show you
His heart and His desires for you. I believe our God
loves to answer those kinds of prayers.

I'm not talking here about grabbing this verse or

*The God Adventure*

that verse out of context and trying to wedge it into your situation to strengthen the case for what you'd already decided to do. What I am talking about is walking through a systematic, daily reading and study of the Bible and doing so with your eyes and ears open to what the Lord might want to say to you. You may be reading in Exodus, Ezra, Song of Solomon, Luke, or 2 Peter. Wherever you are, keep reading faithfully and carefully, asking the Lord to make the path clear to you.

I love J. B. Phillips's paraphrase of James 1:5–6. Speaking about seeking God's wisdom, James says,

> And if, in the process, any of you does not know how to meet any particular problem he has only to ask God—who gives generously to all men without making them feel guilty—and he may be quite sure that the necessary wisdom will be given him. But he must ask in sincere faith without secret doubts.

Time and again, the Holy Spirit has brought words of Scripture to my mind that I don't ever remember reading, let alone memorizing. But suddenly, just when I needed them, they shone out across my path and lit my way.

Ask God for His wisdom. Ask Him to confirm, confirm, confirm the potential adventure He has placed on your heart. Remember, He *generously* ladles out such wisdom. Open His Word. And wait on the Holy Spirit to highlight or underline the words on the pages of His book.

## "This Is the Way, Walk in It"

From time to time through the years, God has also brought into my life people who have a prophetic gift—who are able to speak a word from God into my life. Cathy Lechner has been one of those people. An author and speaker, Cathy has employed her distinctive gift as she ministers around the world. I've had the privilege of being with her on numerous times, and she has often spoken a word into my life at key moments.

When I saw that Cathy was scheduled to be on the *700 Club* again soon, I began talking to the Lord about that time with her. I said, *God, I am not going to ask Cathy to pray for me or tell her my situation. But if You have something You want to speak to me through her, please have her deliver that to me.*

The interview went well, as it always does with

Cathy, and we talked about ministry, world events, family, and a daily walk with Jesus Christ. Then we said our good-byes, and she began to walk off the set. I couldn't help feeling a tiny bit of disappointment in my heart. I had quietly hoped that God might give Cathy a word for me.

Just before she reached the door, Cathy stopped and turned around. She looked at me and said, "Terry, I don't know what this means, but I believe I have a word for you. This is what I sense God saying to you: 'You have a green light, just go. What you are about to do, do quickly, go about it, and don't let anything stop you. Keep moving, go forward.'" Then she walked out the door.

Those words came back to my heart at crucial times in the adoption process, when all the arrangements bogged down, when huge obstacles loomed, and when Andy and I became discouraged and wondered if we would ever be allowed to wrap our arms around those little girls. *Go. Don't let anything stop you. Keep moving. Go forward.* Praise God for that encouragement through His servant!

Having said these things, however, don't just take any prophetic word that comes your way from some traveling minister or casual acquaintance. Make sure that the individual has a deep and consistent walk with

God and that whatever word he or she brings fits right in stride with the commands and counsel of Scripture. But in Cathy's case, I knew the source. I knew her faithfulness to Christ, the quality of her prayer life, and her warmth and friendship for me. What she told me fit hand in glove with what the Lord had already been telling me through circumstances, through close Christian friends, and through my reading of God's Word.

One night as we were struggling with the whole process, I lay in bed wide awake, feeling utterly overwhelmed with all the circumstances. Through my tears, I whispered to the Lord, "I can't do this, God. This is too big, and I'm too little. I don't have what it takes, and I want my life back."

When we talk to the Lord, pouring out our heart, should we really be surprised when He speaks back to us? And that night He did. In the midst of my pain and anxiety and fear, He spoke clearly to my heart with these words: *You are NOT going to do this, Terry. I am. You're going to do it with Me, one day at a time, and that's your secret.* Those words went absolutely cross-grain to what I had been thinking and feeling for hours. Right in the middle of my trauma as I was, I could not have come up with that truth. I was too caught up in emotion, anxiety of heart, and the recognition of my own weakness and inabilities. But cutting right through that fog of confusion and worry, God dropped that clear word of promise into my heart, and immediately I was able to receive it and grab hold of it. The anxiety melted away from me and I fell into peaceful sleep.

No, I didn't have what it took to do it. Neither did Andy. But God did. And once again I had that calming, strengthening assurance that this was no adventure of my own making. This was *His* adventure, the plans of *His* heart, and He had simply invited me along for the ride…if I wanted to come. God was doing something of eternal significance, and He was giving me the opportunity to participate.

That realization, my friend, will roll the pressure right off your shoulders. You will begin to recognize (once again) that you have the freedom to simply rest in your Lord and to wait on Him.

## WAIT ON THE LORD

Sometimes God gives you a vision for an adventure with Him that doesn't come to pass for weeks, months, and maybe even years.

Think of Joseph. What kept him? What kept his

hope and faith alive through the betrayal of his own brothers, through the humiliation of being stripped and sold like a piece of meat on the slave market, through the injustice of being falsely accused by a bored, unhappy woman and spending over two years in Pharaoh's prison? Joseph had a vision. That's what kept him. He remembered the dreams of his youth and the promise that—strange and implausible as it may have sounded to him sometimes—one day he would be in an exalted place of rulership.

That young man held onto that vision for all he was worth, and the Lord brought it to pass in a way that was more wonderful than he could have imagined.

We all need a vision from the Lord to buoy us up in times of adversity or discouragement. Ask Him, your Father who loves you, to give you such a vision. Ask Him to give you a glimpse of where He's taking you, what He has in mind for you. It may come as you are reading the Word of God, or through the assurance of a friend, or through the still, small voice of His Spirit, speaking within your heart in the wee hours of the morning.

Hold onto that vision through every storm, and watch the horizon for its fulfillment. When you do that day by day, it's called "waiting on the Lord." This isn't waiting like the kind you do in a grocery line or

*The God Adventure*

stuck in gridlock on the freeway. This is an active waiting. An alert expectation. A hope that is alive and
eager and confident.

And strangely enough, as you wait, Scripture says
that you will actually gain strength!

> Wait for the LORD;
>> be strong and take heart
>> and wait for the LORD.
>>> PSALM 27:14

> We wait in hope for the LORD;
>> he is our help and our shield.
> In him our hearts rejoice,
>> for we trust in his holy name.
>>> PSALM 33:20–21

> Wait for the LORD
>> and keep his way.
> He will exalt you to inherit the land.
>>> PSALM 37:34

That's such wonderful counsel. Wait for the Lord
to give you the vision and the adventure of His choosing. Wait for the Lord to sustain you, guide you, and
supply your needs as you walk into a strange land

where you have never been before. Wait on the Lord to bring rest to your heart when the way becomes hard and your feet become weary. Wait, wait, wait, until He whispers, *"Now."*

And then step out into a God adventure that will change your life forever.

# Let God Be Big

We are confident of all this because of
our great trust in God through Christ.
It is not that we think we can do anything
of lasting value by ourselves.
Our only power and success come from God.
He is the one who has enabled us.

2 CORINTHIANS 3:4-6, NLT

10

A FRIEND OF MINE fretted over his twenty-year-old daughter being out of the country on a yearlong missions trip. Since it was her first extended time away from home, he wondered how she would handle the pressures of loneliness, cultural adjustment, and myriad new challenges.

He needn't have worried.

She told him in an e-mail, "Dad, when I have my worship and prayer times in the morning, my problems and worries sometimes seem bigger than God. But I just keep praying and worshiping until God gets bigger than my problems."

Now there's a young woman wise beyond her years. So many of us never wait that long in His presence. We rush into our days with big, big problems occupying our minds and a God who seems small and inadequate to meet our needs. As the day progresses, we quickly feel overmatched, overwhelmed, and discouraged. Oh, we would never use the words *small* or *inadequate* to describe God. We might say all the right theological things about Him being *all-powerful, all-knowing,* and *sovereign* over everything.

But when it comes right down to believing in a God who is big enough to take us through every challenge of life, our walk doesn't even come close to matching our talk. And part of the reason we shy away from the idea of a God adventure is that we're afraid we'll get in over our head and even God won't be able to pull us out. We focus on our limitations and inadequacies, rather than on the boundless might of the One who calls us.

That's the single biggest reason why you and I miss out on God adventures.

An opportunity to serve the Lord or follow Him on a new course presents itself before us, and we reject it out of hand, with reasoning something like this...

*I've never done anything like that before.*

*I'm not gifted to do such things.*

*I really don't have the time or the money.*

*I'm a cautious person by nature—not a risk taker.*

*I'm afraid I might fail and look ridiculous.*

*The whole idea just overwhelms me—blows my circuit breakers.*

I guess it really boils down to this: Do we believe that our God is the same God that we read about in

Scripture…or do we have a diluted, disinterested, downsized God who can't really be counted on in times of great challenge or great need?

## TWO LITTLE MEN WHO BECAME BIG

Is the God you and I serve and worship today the same God who said He would strengthen Joshua to step into Moses' sandals and lead a nation into war?

> "Haven't I commanded you? Strength!
> Courage! Don't be timid; don't get discouraged.
> GOD, your God, is with you every step you take."
>
> JOSHUA 1:9, *THE MESSAGE*

Joshua didn't have to be "big." He didn't have to be mighty and commanding and a swaggering military strategist. He knew how to be little so that God could be big. In fact, Joshua was never stronger, never "bigger" than when he "fell facedown to the ground in reverence" before the commander of the Lord's angelic army and said, "What message does my Lord have for his servant?" (Joshua 5:14).

God wanted Joshua to understand that He was not

going to share the stage. But if Joshua would be fully obedient and step out in courage and faith, mighty things would happen—events that would be told and retold for thousands of years.

Many centuries later, the prophet Jeremiah found himself in a situation that must have seemed like the end of the world. Babylon, the world superpower at the time, had conquered all of Judah. And now the Babylonian army was in the process of building siege ramps along the city walls of Jerusalem. It was only a matter of time before that powerful army breached the walls and destroyed the city.

Zedekiah, king of Judah, hated Jeremiah's prophecies of Jerusalem's imminent fall. Rather than heeding the prophet's warnings, he had Jeremiah shoved into a high-walled courtyard and locked in. In the meantime, God had given Jeremiah a bewildering, confusing message—instructing him to count out money and buy property in a city that was about to be leveled and occupied for who knows how many years by an invading army.

A sensitive man, Jeremiah must have been at his wits' end. Can't you just see him slumping against the walls of that dusty little courtyard? The world was falling down around him, all the foundations were shaken. He could hear the sounds of the Babylonians constructing their ramps. He had preached his heart out, but everyone ignored his message and despised him for saying it. Then he was thrown into a prison and locked up all by himself. And to top it all, the God he served had given him instructions that seemed wildly contradictory and made no sense at all.

His problems were BIG. Very, very big. His frustration and anxiety levels must have been at the max. But what do you do when your problems have grown so big that you can't even see over them or around them?

You let God be even bigger. Because He is.

Alone and seemingly abandoned in that empty courtyard, Jeremiah got down on his knees and began to pray. "Ah Lord GOD! Behold, You have made the heavens and the earth by Your great power and by Your outstretched arm! Nothing is too difficult for You" (Jeremiah 32:17, NASB).

It really didn't matter that men had locked him up and thrown away the key. It didn't matter that the greatest army in the world was within striking distance of his city and his home. It didn't matter that he found God's ways beyond his understanding. *He had a God who had created the universe! Nothing in all this world was too difficult for such a God!*

And when he prayed in that way, God replied with these words: "Behold, I am the LORD, the God of all flesh; is anything too difficult for Me?" (v. 27, NASB). A little later, God came to him and said, "Call to me and I will answer you and tell you great and unsearchable things you do not know" (33:3).

In other words, God was saying, "You have that right, Jeremiah. You see Me as I am. And I am every bit as big as you see Me. I'm about to do mighty things that will shake the world. But because You believe in Me and trust in Me, just call on Me whenever you want to, and I will walk with you, have fellowship with you, and share My secrets with you."

And so it is with you and me. God *will* work out His kingdom purposes for our world. And if He invites you to participate with Him in those purposes, He *will* be responsible to provide whatever it takes for you to accomplish what He calls you to do. The smaller we make ourselves in the process, the bigger He will be for us.

That's a hard thing for most of us to accept. All of our lives we've been raised to pull ourselves up by our bootstraps and say, "I can do this. I can make it through this." We've been taught to push, to excel, to achieve, to grab for the gusto, to climb the ladder, and to "reach for the stars" (whatever *that* means).

But God's kingdom purposes are the reverse of man's. God tells us, "Man looks on the outward appearance, but I look on the heart. I don't care what you look like. I don't care about your assessment of your own abilities. I don't care about your title or your resume. I don't care how many times you have tried and failed before. I don't care about how many degrees or honors you have behind your name. What I want to see is men and women who will let Me be big in their lives."

## THERE FOR THE ASKING

As difficult as it may be for us to believe sometimes, God is speaking to us, reaching out to us, wanting to have a relationship with us. As with Jeremiah, He wants us to call to Him so that He can show us great and mighty things. It's there for the asking! It's there for those who will bow down, put their faces to the ground, and say, "God, help me to be little so that You can be big in my life."

Yes, you can be a believer and never really think about His greatness and your own smallness in His presence. But you will miss out on what you were created for! And when you try to walk into a God adventure, you will be overwhelmed and discouraged and may find yourself turning back.

*The God Adventure*

Making yourself small before the Lord really means that you exalt His agenda before your own. You are surrendering to Him your understanding, your purposes, and your dreams. That doesn't mean "giving up" your hopes or dreams. Not at all. It's just that we need to hold them with open hands before Him, instead of clinging to them with white knuckles. We say to Him, "Lord, You know my dreams. But if Your dream is different for me than my dream, then I'm giving You permission to change my dream. I'm giving You permission to do the unexpected, even to do what seems terrifying to me right now. Whatever Your purpose is, God, I want to be a part of it."

Now you can do that in one of two ways. You can surrender to Him with gritted teeth, grimly buckling your seatbelt and hanging on for the ride, expecting that it's going to cost you—that God's going to ask you to do something you don't want to do and will probably make you miserable for life. Or, you can surrender with a sense of awe and expectation, believing that His purposes for you are good, that He wants to give you a future and a hope, and that He's going to shape and form you into all that He created you to be.

And so, my friend, you can expect awesome, incredible, impossible-to-imagine things in your future as you surrender to Him moment by moment, day by day, struggle by struggle, and dream by dream.

It's an adventure all right and a plunge into mystery. But don't be afraid. He is the Great Shepherd, and He is not going to let anything happen to you that you and He together can't handle. He is able to accomplish all that concerns you today and to blend your life into a mighty plan that will outlast the stars and bring glory to His name forever.

It's such an amazing irony, isn't it? The smaller you make yourself in His presence, the more He will be able to use you in the greatest of ways. The lower you bow, the higher He will exalt you. The more you surrender, the greater your reward. There's really nothing about a God adventure that makes much human sense.

Not now, anyway. But someday it will. Someday, we will marvel.

# A Detour in the Desert

*"I remember the devotion of your youth...*
*how you followed me in the wilderness,*
*in a land not sown."*

JEREMIAH 2:2, ESV

11

GOD ADVENTURES are for those who sense His sovereign, guiding hand on the events of their lives—even when those events seem overwhelming or come wrapped in distress and pain. These are the people who understand that the journey to higher usefulness and greater blessing in Christ's kingdom will sometimes make a detour through the wilderness.

That makes more sense when life is calm and peaceful than it does when the roof caves in. In times of setbacks and crushing circumstances, it's not always so easy to remember the "adventure" side of things.

Have you ever wished you could go back in time and counsel yourself? Most of us who have lived very long can look back on times when sorrow weighed heavy upon us, and we felt all alone with our pain. We can remember certain days and certain hours when we were so paralyzed by fear, torn by anguish, or broken by disappointment that we wanted to die—or maybe curl up in a fetal position on the floor and just stay like that for hours.

If you've never been in such a place, you are blessed. Praise God for the grace upon your life. If you have been there, you know exactly what I'm talking about. You can close your eyes right now and see yourself as a child, tears streaming down your cheeks, walking home from school with rejection aching in your young soul. You can see yourself slumped on your couch, many years later, with your face in your hands—so lonely, so lost. Or maybe you have a mental film clip of yourself walking a long, empty beach on a gray afternoon, wishing you could just walk and walk until the end of the world.

What if you could go back to your past self in such moments and speak a few words of comfort or hope? What would you say? *Don't cry, little girl. It's going to be all right. Your best friend will come back to you. She really loves you best.* Or maybe, *You're going to survive this, young woman. This won't last forever. Life will be sweet again. It hurts now—I know it hurts! But don't give up! Reach out to God.*

If it were me, I would talk about an eternal perspective and God's good purposes in my life. I would explain as gently as I could that even the most terrible wilderness can be the beginning of a God adventure. I would say, "Terry, I know it seems awfully black right now—as black as it's ever been for you. I know what you're thinking—that there isn't any way out of this mess. But listen—this *will* pass. I promise you. And out of this pain and grief you're enduring, God is going to accomplish something very, very special in your life."

I would go back and talk to the young Terry who had just been raped. And I would tell her that out of the ashes of her self-sufficiency and proud self-seeking, she would find the True Love of her life…and a fresh purpose for living.

I would sit with the Terry who had just experienced a crushing divorce and felt so near despair. I would try to convince her that she would grow through this darkest of hours and find a walk with God that she had never experienced before. And then I would smile and give her just a little glimpse of a wonderful husband on up ahead—and seven children!

That is probably just what the Counselor, the Holy Spirit, wants to do in our lives in times of trial. He knows what's ahead. He knows the plans He has for us. He knows what He intends to accomplish in us and through us. And He knows that the path through the wilderness is really the best way Home.

## Unfolding the Map

God uses those wilderness experiences. And they come into the life of every human being on this broken planet. Imagine you could look down on the life of a man or woman and see it as a road map, covering birth to departure. You could see the road wind through green areas with parks and blue waters. As you unfold the map panel by panel, you would note those dotted lines along the route that denote "scenic highways," where life overflows with wonder and beauty. Unfold a few more panels and you'll see those stark white places on the map where the road winds through…nothing. Just emptiness and desolation, without any picnic areas, points of interest, or cheerful streams—and not so much as a tree on the horizon.

Our family entered such a barren place a number of years ago. Our financial problems had gone from bad to worse to critical! For the first and only time in our lives, we found ourselves walking very, very near the cliff-edge of bankruptcy.

Distressed and anxious, we worried about all of those scary what-ifs that now loomed on our horizon. *Would we have to move? But we didn't want to move! We were so comfortable! We were near both sets of grandparents, had a wonderful church and a terrific group of Christian friends.*

And yet...

Our Father used that wilderness experience to uproot us and relocate us here in Virginia...where we have found ministry opportunities beyond what we had ever dreamed. Frankly, I don't see how we would have ever moved otherwise. We loved our neighborhood, our town, our church, and we lived in a home we'd dreamed of for years and built with our own hands.

But heaven had an adventure in mind for us on up the road. And if you sense God leading out in front of you, it's no time to sit still! The first leg of that adventure, however, plunged us right into the wilderness. God took us into the desert places in order to bring us to a new and even better place and a wider, more fruitful era in our lives. We couldn't have guessed. We wouldn't have known. But the God of tomorrow was out ahead of us, preparing magnificent opportunities and experiences.

In Ezekiel 20:10, God says of His people, "I brought them out and led them into the desert" (CEV).

And He did so because it was the very path to the Land of Promise.

## LONG DETOUR

Remember that road map of life I spoke of? Wouldn't it be interesting to unfold King David's map on the table? What a ride he had! From shepherd boy to national hero to son-in-law of the king. What an elevation gain in such a short space! Could he go much higher?

Yes, he could. But not yet.

Even though he had been anointed as king, the highway of his life plunged from green pastures and still waters into the most desolate of wastelands. In these lonely, forgotten, windswept haunts on the back side of Israel, the king-designate ran from rock to rock, cave to cave, hiding from the jealous madman Saul. For *fifteen years!*

In those difficult, soul-testing years, David learned to wait upon the Lord. Like a cypress tree that seems to spring right out of the rock, David sent his roots deep and tasted what it meant to draw upon God's wisdom and power.

And one little side note. As a result of that detour through the desert, we have psalms that sustain us—like sweet, cold water from a deep desert spring—in our own times of disappointment and sorrow.

> When my spirit grows faint within me,
>> it is you who know my way....
> I spread out my hands to you;
>> my soul thirsts for you like a parched land....
> Show me the way I should go,
>> for to you I lift up my soul.
>> PSALM 142:3; 143:6, 8

That future ministry isn't something David could have anticipated in his own lifetime. But God did. God has the map of all of our lives spread out before Him. And God knew that out of David's lean, fugitive years, a mighty hymnbook of Israel would find some of its most powerful anthems. And millions upon millions of hurting saints would be encouraged to cling to their God and look to Him for direction in the long, dark passages of life.

See? It isn't always about us! There may be purposes in our trials and suffering that we may never discover in this life—and that will outlast our lives tenfold. Our God is the God of today and tomorrow.

No one can say for sure, but I think there's a good

chance that David learned more about God and grew more in his faith during those fifteen years of exile than he did in the many subsequent years he sat on a throne.

We could say the same of Joseph, in the book of Genesis. His years of slavery, unjust accusation, and imprisonment did more to strengthen his spirit and deepen his walk with God than decades as the coruler of Egypt. Of those hard and bitter days, the Bible tells us, "His feet were hurt with fetters; his neck was put in a collar of iron" (Psalm 105:18, ESV). And that iron went into his soul!

God strengthened him for a huge task that would have been beyond his imagination in those dark days of trial after trial. And after years on the throne, God gave him the perspective to say to the very brothers who had despised him and sold him into slavery, "As for you, you meant evil against me; but God meant it for good" (Genesis 50:20, NKJV).

God will take your wilderness experiences— whether you are there by your own poor choices or by God's wise design—and He will use them for greatness in your life, if you allow Him to.

But first you have to recognize His presence with you, and His power to use present events to mold you for future opportunities and blessings.

## Decisions in the Desert

We have very dear friends, both in the ministry, who have been through a profound wilderness experience over this past year. Out of the blue, he was diagnosed with a rare and virulent form of cancer. In an effort to save him, the doctors performed surgery after debilitating surgery that could have taken his life. Sparing that, the surgeries could have easily taken his ability to taste and eat—or his voice, which would have ended his evangelistic ministry and the great passion of his life.

In God's mercy, however, he walked out of that wilderness alive and whole. More than that, he emerged a much stronger man, with a deeper faith than he had ever experienced. "Our marriage," his wife told me, "has never been what it is today. It's so much better. And our children have grown in their faith and their walk with God." Everyone who knows him recognizes a new power in his preaching and teaching.

I said to them, "I can see it in you. I can see it all. But I don't want to go through what you've gone through to get there!"

We all laughed and ended up concluding that God doesn't give us a choice about entering the wilderness. We don't get to say when or where or how long. But He does allow us to choose how we will respond. Will it be the first leg in a life-shaping God adventure, or will it simply harden us and drive us deeper into ourselves, distracting us from the Kingdom purposes intended for our lives?

It's true, the call to adventure, change, and new paths in the Christian life often begins with a wilderness experience. Perhaps it's because we learn to cling to Him for dear life in those days of dark storms and withering heat. *The shadow of a mighty rock within a weary land,* as the old hymn describes it. He brings us to the place where we have to rely on Him just to survive. And standing in that comforting shadow, clinging to Him, listening for His voice, we begin to understand more of who He is and His desires for our lives.

You cannot change the timing of your entrance into the wilderness, nor the duration of your stay. But you can accept these times as from the hand of the Lord. David realized that all of life—even those hard and heartbreaking seasons—was in God's hand. In Psalm 31 he wrote: "But I trust in you, O LORD; I say, 'You are my God.' My times are in Your hand" (vv. 14–15).

When I talk about accepting these things, I don't mean a fatalistic, grit-your-teeth-and-bear-it kind of acceptance, but rather a way that makes you more sensitive to God's voice. *What is this all about, Lord? What do You want me to learn? What is it You're wanting to*

*change in me? I give You free reign to do that. Help me to*
*respond to You in these hard times!*

That's not an easy thing to do. It requires walking
hand in hand with Him, leaning hard upon Him, and
drawing upon His power to take the next step…and
the next, and the next. We must wait upon Him for
that. I believe that's what Isaiah 40 is talking about
when it says,

> Those who wait on the LORD
> Shall renew their strength;
> They shall mount up with wings like eagles,
> They shall run and not be weary,
> They shall walk and not faint.
>
> V. 31, NKJV

I have a wonderful friend named Stephanie
Seefeldt who is a gifted singer and songwriter. There's a
lyric in one of her songs that I really love. She sings,
*"When you do not know the way God leads, you will
know your God."*

And that's the strongest preparation for those
inevitable wilderness detours that I can think of. Know
your God. Be in the Word. Walk with Him. Listen to
what He's speaking to your heart. Get away from the
noise and activity, and spend quiet time alone with

Him. *Know* Him, so that when the trials and tribulations come and you don't understand His leading or the things that are happening to you, you can hang on strongly to who you know Him to be.

Don't wait for the hard times! Don't wait for the wilderness! Make a practice of clinging to Him now so that when your path plunges into a dark canyon, you won't have to grope for His hand. You'll already be holding it.

# A Final Question

Live life, then, with a due sense of responsibility,

not as men who do not know the meaning

and purpose of life but as those who do.

Make the best use of your time,

despite all the difficulties of these days.

Don't be vague, but firmly grasp what

you know to be the will of the Lord.

EPHESIANS 5:15–17, PHILLIPS

12

REMEMBER THAT mysterious word picture from the book of Ezekiel that so captured my heart? There was the angel of the Lord, stepping out of that vision, glowing like molten metal, and leading the prophet deeper and deeper into the clear water gushing from a future temple in Jerusalem. First up to his ankles. Then up to his knees. Then as high as his waist. And then...over his head and "deep enough to swim in."

That night at the Art Katz meeting so many years ago, the Lord called me to leave my safe shoreline and venture into deeper places than I had ever been before. He was calling me to get in over my head, where I couldn't touch bottom, where I couldn't rely on myself or be in control. It was terrifying, and it was wonderful.

When I met Andy, I found a man with that same heart. Before we married, we vowed to each other that we would be risk takers for the Lord. As time went by, we adopted two children in addition to our two biological children. And then when the door opened to change the life of three young Ukrainian girls…we walked into a God adventure that continues to this day.

Life hasn't been a cakewalk by any means. There have been seasons of stress and anxiety and pressure. But as far as Andy and I are concerned, there's only one thing worse than a difficult life…and that's an irrelevant life. A life lived in the safe, tepid shallows. A life that doesn't make any difference at all.

In Luke 5:4, Jesus told His disciples to launch out into the deep and let down their nets. I'm sure it had been a very long night already, and these men were discouraged as well as weary. It doesn't take much imagination to picture them dirty, grumpy, cramped from hours in the boat, and hungry on top of that. It was a stretch for them to row out to deeper waters and throw that net one more time.

Maybe that's where you are with all this "God adventure" talk. You're thinking, *That's all well and good for you, Terry, and for those other people you've mentioned. But I've been at this place before, tried launching out, and it didn't work for me. I started with empty nets, and I ended with empty nets.*

Could it be that you undertook a task that originated with yourself, rather than Him? Was it something of your own making? Believe me, there is a huge difference. A God adventure isn't something you "do for God." It isn't even something *you* decide to do at all. A God adventure is something God is already doing, and He invites you to join Him. In other words, the heavenly bus is already rolling, heading for a destination. It stops (maybe just for a few moments) in front of your house, the door swings open, and you can either get on board or let the door close and watch the bus disappear into the distance.

There may be other buses, but that bus is gone. You'll never have another opportunity to experience that particular adventure again.

This is something that is God's idea, God's initiative. And though you may have tried something similar on your own in the past, this is very, very different. You're on God's bus. He's behind the wheel and He knows where He is going. The way may be dark or foggy, so that you can't see much out of the windows, but you can count on the fact that your driver never forgets His destination.

> There has never been the slightest doubt in my mind that the God who started this great work in you would keep at it and bring it to a flourishing finish on the very day Christ Jesus appears.
>
> PHILIPPIANS 1:6, THE MESSAGE

For the disciples, the difference between a self-generated enterprise and a God adventure was very clear. At the end of a long, long night of fishing, they had caught nothing. But somewhere near dawn, on a short excursion into deeper water at the word of a Stranger on shore, they found more fish than their nets could contain. Isn't that interesting? It was the same lake, the same boat, the same men, and the same nets. But when Jesus was directing things, the results couldn't even be compared.

That's the way it is when God leads you into one of His expeditions of faith. You will find your nets overflowing, and they will not tear. You'll discover that you have everything you need to accomplish the task, and you will marvel at what you see God accomplishing in you and through you. You'll also know beyond the shadow of a doubt that it was not of your doing.

I've subscribed to several devotional e-mail services that pop up on my computer screen from time to time. Not long ago, I saw this little message from the pen of Ras Robinson and a ministry called The Fullness Network. The words are written as though God Himself was speaking to the reader:

Launch out into the deep. You have done well, but you have been fishing in the shallows....

There are much bigger fish to be caught—but you have to go beyond what you can see with your own eyes. There will be uncertainty in your heart if you decide to go forward with Me. Many times you will feel lost and without a compass. Clouds will roll in and block your view of the heavens. No certain human navigation is available to you. At this point you will cast yourself upon My mercy, and you will then be launched into your eternal destiny, going far beyond the shallows. You were never made to remain in the shallows. I say unto you, sail the high seas and gain the full reward of pinpoint obedience. *Launch out into the deep.*

Why did the Lord send His men back for one last dip of the net? To begin with, He simply wanted them to find success in their hearts' desire, in the activity they were gifted and trained to do. But He wanted them to do it with Him, in Him, and out of obedience to Him. He wanted them to recognize that it was His power in them and His blessing upon them that achieved results, not their own purpose and desire.

## Expect the Unexpected

Jesus was always doing the unexpected, wasn't He? He spit into dirt, took the mud, and smeared it on a blind man's eyes. He blessed a wedding party by turning six kegs of tap water into fine Cabernet. He flabbergasted the religious elite by dining with drunks, prostitutes, and a whole assortment of unsavory citizens. No one could predict what He would do next.

He's still doing the unexpected today. He still stuns and perplexes people. He still turns things upside down and inside out. He still leads daring raids into enemy territory, freeing hostages, releasing prisoners, and confounding the battle plans of hell. He still loves using weak, failing, unlikely men and women to win great victories in His name.

And He invites us to join Him. God is calling us to step into areas beyond our control, over our heads, and way outside the boundaries of our comfort and confidence. That's often the very place where His work lies. The question is, will you come along?

Do you have to? Will He compel you to? Absolutely not. As the old hymn puts it, "Whosoever will may come." You don't have to step out and follow Him into the realms of uncertainty. But there is a cost if you don't. And who could quantify such a cost?

*A Final Question*

Who can put a price tag on lost vision, diminished faith, forfeited blessings, or years of stagnation and wandering in the wilderness?

My friend tells a story from his boyhood in the 1950s, about his next-door neighbors. Ed Crom answered his phone late one night, and the operator said he had a collect call from Scotland. Back then people calling collect could give one or two words, stating who they were or why they were calling. In this case, the one word was "inheritance."

Ed Crom refused the call. It may not have bothered him very much, but when my friend heard about it, it nearly drove him crazy. How could Mr. Crom *do* that? How could he turn his back on that word, that tantalizing hint, that promise, that mystery, that intriguing connection to a land beyond the sea? Okay, so what if it had turned out to be a hoax or a dead end or a lot of nothing? Wasn't it worth a few dollars to see what might lie behind such an invitation?

*A castle?*

*A wide, windswept estate in the Scottish hills?*

*A family treasure?*

*An exciting connection to some wonderful mystery in the British Isles?*

Ed Crom will never know. He went to his grave not knowing, because there were no following calls or letters, and he never heard about it again.

In the same way, you and I will never know, per-haps until we stand before the judgment seat of Christ, what might have been, what could have happened, if we had swallowed our fears, tossed aside our cautions, and taken a ride down roads of mystery and wonder with the God of the universe.

The best news of all is this. If you're still breathing, it's not too late to enter into adventures in faith. It's not too late to step into His mighty purposes. You may have missed the mark before, but today is today. And with Paul we can say,

> No dear brothers and sisters, I am still not all I
> should be, but I am focusing all my energies on
> this one thing: Forgetting the past and looking
> forward to what lies ahead, I strain to reach the
> end of the race and receive the prize for which
> God, through Christ Jesus, is calling us up to
> heaven.
>
> PHILIPPIANS 3:13–14, NLT

What a wonderful hope! God says, "Forget the past. Don't waste a single minute mourning over missed opportunities. The prize is still there to be won! The goal is still out ahead. There is still time to go for it and to move into His purposes and His calling."

Here is what I think: I think God would love to have you join Him, starting today, in all kinds of amazing and unlikely adventures. He would love to show you His power. He would love to use you and bless you as you've never been used and blessed before.

## "WE'RE ALL WATCHING YOU"

Whether you realize it or not, your decisions in this area will affect more people than yourself. Why? Because people are watching. And you have no idea when or who. Your kids wonder how much you really believe what you've taught them about God and if you're willing to step out in faith and trust Him to take care of you. Your neighbors wonder if you're just another dress-up-on-Sunday religious person and if your beliefs have anything to do with everyday life. Your coworkers are looking for an excuse to blow off your Christianity and aren't sure you really believe what you say you believe.

People wonder if God really exists. People wonder if God is truly good. People wonder if God actually reaches down and interacts with people—if He truly cares about what's going on in our lives. And how will they discover these things if they don't read the Bible and they don't go to church? They'll discover it as they watch you give yourself to God adventures and live by faith.

Other believers are watching us, too.

Back when we were still walking through the adoption, I remember sharing our struggles with an acquaintance of mine. I told her about some of the setbacks and roadblocks we had encountered and how God had faithfully removed them, one by one. We talked about the challenges that still faced us: These were children we really knew nothing about. We didn't know their background or how they felt about leaving the Ukraine and coming to America. We knew they didn't speak English and undoubtedly carried some emotional baggage from their past.

All of these things were part of our God adventure and we were waiting on Him day by day to guide us and provide for us. As we parted and said good-bye, I'll never forget what happened. She walked a few steps and then turned around and said, "We're all watching you." And with that she waved and walked away.

Her comment stopped me dead in my tracks. I thought to myself, *Goodness, what kind of responsibility is that? To think that people are watching how this unfolds in our lives. They're watching how we handle it. They're watching to see how God will come through.*

In that moment, I just cried out to the Lord. I said, *Lord, we can't make this happen. And even if we could, we don't want to make this happen. I can't speak into this woman's life or anybody else's. If this is all going to take place, God, You're the one who has to pull it off. In fact, Lord, I'm turning around and watching You, just as she says she is watching me. I'm waiting and watching to see how You are going to do this.*

It was one of those moments of surrender when you say, "God, this is all about You." When you do that, when you give your adventure right back to God, He has a freedom to work in it and to walk it out in you and through you. People see this happening before their eyes. They see what He is doing and that even though you are far from perfect, you are truly a work in process.

## "What Do You Want Me to Do?"

Picture Saul of Tarsus, facedown in the dirt and gravel of the Damascus road, his eyes seared by a brightness greater than the sun at noonday. Jesus had just turned Saul's carefully ordered world on its ear. Everything he had poured his life into exploded in that instant. His assumptions had been dead wrong. His persecution of this "Jesus sect" had been a terrible injustice and a great offense to heaven. He had been fighting the very God he thought he had been serving.

In a time such as that, Saul's question was probably the most logical one possible: *"Lord, what do You want me to do?"* (Acts 9:6, NKJV). It's the best question for you and me, too. Really, you can't find a better question than that.

No matter who you are or where you have been up to this point in your life, God wants to invite you out into a deeper adventure with Him. It doesn't matter if you're in middle school or a nursing home. The truth is, God adventures await around every corner.

And God is waiting for obedient, willing hearts— men and women who are willing to go wherever and do whatever, in response to His call. *"Lord, what do You want me to do?"*

Can you imagine starting each day of your life with words like these?

"Lord, if Your bus stops in front of my house or my school or my office today, I'm getting in. Show me what You want me to do. Open my eyes to the opportunities before me. Here I am, Lord. Let's go on an adventure together."

Don't be afraid to say that to Him. Don't be afraid of what God might call you to do. He is abundantly able to keep you in the place He has led you. If you're going to fear something, be afraid of finding yourself stuck where God doesn't want you to be. Be afraid of missing His blessing. Be afraid of losing the vision. Be afraid of spending your one life on this earth on the sidelines.

But don't be afraid of the God adventure. Don't be afraid when He calls you into the deep with Him.

You'll never learn to swim in two inches of water.

Launch out! You were created for this!

Twenty percent of the proceeds of this book will go to assist adoptions, orphanages, and orphans transitioning into adulthood.
For more information go to www.terrymeeuwsen.com.